Contents

The Canal Boat Manual is published by *Canal Boat & Inland Waterways* magazine, Britain's brightest waterways monthly

Subscriptions hotline 0870 830 4960
www.canalboatmag.co.uk

Editor	Kevin Blick
Sub-editor	Jayne Gardner
Contributors	David Addison, Tony Brooks, Mark Langley, David Pullen
Photography	David Oakes, Derek Pratt, Martin Ludgate, Phillippa Greenwood, Jo May
Editorial tel: 01799 544200	Email: editor@canalboatmag.co.uk
Advertisement Manager	Jennifer Raby
Advertising sales	Claire Randall
Advertising tel: 0118 989 7242	Email: ads@canalboatmag.co.uk

Published by ARCHANT } SPECIALIST

The Mill, Bearwalden Business Park, Wendens Ambo, Essex CB11 4GB

Executive director	Derek Barnes
Managing director	Farine Clarke

Design & origination by APC Graphics, Unit 3 Leanne Business Centre, Sandford Lane, Wareham, Dorset BH20 4DY
Printed by Williams Press, Maidenhead, Berkshire
© Archant Specialist 2006

Where to cruise

Britain's canals and rivers offer enormous variety and interest. We look at our glorious waterway heritage

Arguably the ultimate canal challenge, the 29 locks of the Caen Hill flight on the Kennet and Avon Canal

Britain's waterways are a different world. You can explore them on foot, by bike or just sit on a bankside and fish or enjoy a pint – but the best way to really discover the waterways and their secrets is by boat.

Over 50,000 boats are based on Britain's waterways. It might sound a lot, but when you consider they share more than 4000 miles of water – and that only a small proportion are on the move at any one time – you can understand how boating remains the perfect way to get away from the bustle of the modern world. Especially as you'll rarely be travelling much more than walking pace.

In the *Canal Boat* Manual we will be taking you through the whole process of choosing and buying a boat but first, it's time to say something more about the waterways you will be cruising on.

Today's waterways are used almost exclusively for leisure. You will often find yourself sharing a lock with fellow holidaymakers: only rarely with a freight barge. But the reason we have so many water routes to enjoy is because, hundreds of years ago, these were the freight-carrying motorways of their day.

RIVER NAVIGATIONS
Our major rivers such as the Thames, Trent and Severn as well as many of our smaller local waterways

have been navigated since pre-history, moving cargo from the countryside and the mines to towns, and cities or inland from the coastal ports. Boats would be either sailing craft (such as Thames sailing barges and Severn trows) or horse-drawn. On some rivers, they would even be physically hauled by gangs of men.

In the early days, boats had to work with the flow of current and tide but medieval times saw the first works being carried out to ease the sometimes hard task of navigating upstream against the current with the introduction of crude 'flash locks', little more than a removable gate in a weir through which a boat could be hauled.

In the 16th century, a new invention emerged – the 'pound lock'. This comprised a brick or turf-lined chamber with gates at each end, which could be filled from the river above or emptied into the river below. The boatman would manoeuvre his craft into the lock when empty; close the bottom gates; fill the lock; then open the top gates and leave at the upper level. The same system is still used today, 450 years on.

THE COMING OF THE CANALS
A canal is an artificial, man-made waterway. Britain's first was dug by the Romans (the Fossdyke Navigation, from the River Trent to Lincoln). The vast majority, however, were built in the late 18th and early 19th centuries, as the magnates of the industrial revolution sought a new, cheaper way to transport coal and other raw materials around the country. Great engineers of the period like James Brindley and Thomas Telford were employed to build them.

Canals criss-crossed the country, even extending into such unlikely rural areas as the Brecon Beacons and deepest Somerset. No fewer than three canals cross the country over the challenging terrain of the Pennines – hardly ideal canal-building territory.

Canals are, of course, far from unique to this country but the system that evolved during this period makes our canals a very significant part of our industrial heritage. Many were designed to link to existing river navigations and so create through routes right across the country. The result is a large and intricately linked inland waterway network which provides almost endless cruising possibilities today.

The canals' industrial heyday was brief. By 1850,

The spectacular Pontcysyllte Aqueduct is a wonder of the canal age

Today's canals run past modern industry as well as relics of the old which they were built to serve

Big skies, wide, flat countryside and lock-free rivers characterise the Fenland waterways

Eerie tunnels, like Harecastle Tunnel here, are a particular feature of our canals

railways were the "coming thing" and canals fell into a long decline. Many were officially abandoned or simply fell into dereliction. The trend began to be reversed in the 1950s, when a far-sighted band of enthusiasts launched a campaign to revive and re-open these unloved backwaters.

Their success has led to a boom in pleasure boating. Canalside industrial areas and city centre watersides have been revived for leisure and residential use, while long-lost canals have been re-opened and campaigns to restore others are well underway.

CRUISING TODAY

The most significant feature of inland boating on our waterway system is that on the 'narrow' canals of central England boat size is limited by lock dimensions, usually to 72ft length and 7ft wide. From this evolved the 'narrowboat' as we know it, which is the only craft, other than small day boats and specially made narrow cruisers, which can cruise the whole connected network. (Actually 72ft long narrowboats cannot cruise some of the northern canals where locks, though wide, are restricted in length. The longest 'go-absolutely-anywhere' boat is therefore about 60ft long.)

In effect the inland system is (for the foreseeable future at least) separated into three broad divisions, between which only narrowboats can pass. There are plans to link some of these together

but the reality is likely to be many years away.

The 'southern and western waterways Central to these is the River Thames on which can be found everything from ocean freighters to tiny canoes. Traditionally its affluent home counties stretches have been home to the large 'gin palace' cruisers but their waterspace is increasingly being invaded by the narrowboat.

From the Thames, the quiet, National Trust owned River Wey runs to the south, leading to the Basingstoke Canal, sadly regularly shut for lack of water. The widebeam Kennet & Avon canal leaves the Thames at Reading and runs to Bath and Bristol. (Experienced and suitably equipped boaters can venture further into the Bristol Channel to reach the River Avon and travel as far as Stratford and Stourport.)

Two other canals link with the Thames: the Grand Union Canal leaves the Thames at Brentford and is usable by widebeam boats as far north as Birmingham and the GU and Regents Canal provide a route across north London to the Thames again at Limehouse or north east onto the rivers Lee and Stort, while the narrow Oxford Canal meets it at Oxford.

The East Anglian waterways The River Great Ouse and its tributaries (the best known being the River Cam which can be explored to Cambridge) together with the largely man-made drainage channels that make up the Middle Level

create a fascinating series of waterways through the Fenland landscape.

There is a through route to the canal system via the Middle Level and River Nene but only narrowboats can make the final section along a narrow stretch of the Grand Union. The Ouse is navigable to Bedford at present but there are long term plans to create a link through to the GU. Likewise there is a project to make a through link from the River Witham at the bottom end.

The Northern waterways Wider beam boats can traverse huge areas of the northern waterways, from Boston in the east, to York, Manchester and Liverpool. Sizeable rivers dominate the system, notably the Trent and its tributaries the Soar and Witham, which span the east Midlands and up to Hull, and the Yorkshire Ouse through York and Ripon. From these, wide canals like the Aire & Calder, Leeds & Liverpool and restored Rochdale cross the Pennines to Lancashire.

Traditionally the differing styles of waterway would have been populated by different styles of boat – the sturdy steel narrowboat was a natural vessel to tackle the locks of the canals while the lighter and faster cruiser was happiest and most capable on the open spaces and flowing currents of rivers. Today, though, many boaters explore both the rivers and the canal system in one boat – and it is the narrowboat whose popularity has grown and spread.

River cruising still has a very different feel to

Rivers, like the Avon seen here at Evesham, are usually wider and have fewer locks

The delightful Shropshire Union is one of our most picturesque canals

canal boating. In essence, river cruising takes place on a much larger canvas. The locks and bridges are wider, the channel deeper and broader. There are generally fewer locks, and on rivers like the Thames, all the locks are operated for you by full-time lock-keepers.

With many riverside towns and villages, river boating often has a strong social element and is especially popular with regular weekend boaters. Small grp boats can be very inexpensive to buy and own, and many can be trailed behind a car.

The shallower, man-made channel means that canal cruising is slower than river cruising. You will often cruise at around 3mph (the speed limit is 4mph), whereas river cruisers will typically navigate at 5-6mph. Canal locks are more frequent and rarely automated. On many canals, the locks are grouped together in flights – a run of up to 36 locks in quick succession. Though feared by some novices, locks are part of the fun of canal cruising and most boaters have their own favourites.

ISOLATED WATERWAYS

The coast of our small island is edged with river inlets. Many of these, though unconnected to the main system, are still navigable for varying distances from the coast and have their own boat populations. There are also some disconnected canals, notably South Wales' scenic Monmouthshire & Brecon Canal.

HIRING A BOAT

Hiring a boat for a holiday is a great first step to explore the waterways – or a way for the experienced boater to visit somewhere different.

Boats are available for hire in all shapes and sizes: spacious boats for families, shorter craft for couples, longer ones for large groups; no-frills boats, luxury craft, and all points in between. DVD players, microwaves, and 240v mains are now common features. A star rating system has been introduced to help you choose. Most companies now offer internet booking and availability searches.

Boats are usually hired by the week, but an increasing number of fleets offer three- or four-day short breaks. Though cruising holidays may sometimes seem expensive at first glance, they compare very well when you break the cost down per person, per night. Fuel is included in the price, and on most waterways, overnight mooring is free.

Many hire fleets are small, family-owned operations, but even the larger fleets pride themselves on their personal service. You will be given tuition on the basics of boat handling and (on the canals) lock operation before you set off.

Each operator produces its own brochure, explaining the features of their craft and the cruising routes available from their base. Many hirers choose to follow a 'ring' route taking in several canals and rivers, but an out-and-back holiday can be just as fun: the scenery always looks different on the way back, and you're unlikely to exhaust the supply of pubs. The waterways are best appreciated at a relaxed pace, so resist the temptation to get as many miles under your belt as possible.

Taking a narrowboat up the Thames through London is a memorable narrowboating feat

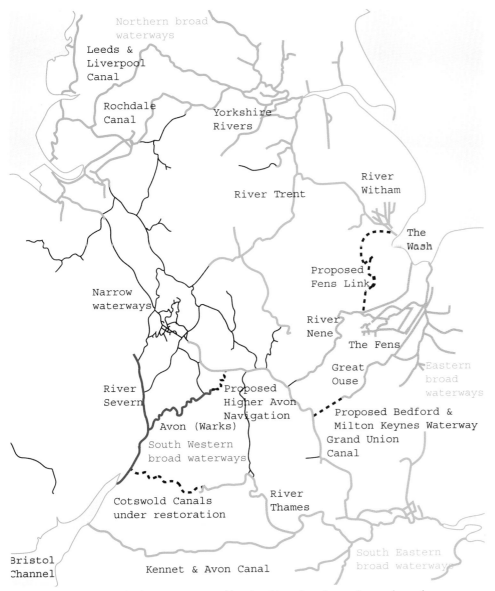

Spectacular scenery on Scotland's Caledonian Canal

A large proportion of the inland waterways is accessible to broad beam boats but, as the map shows, the vital linking sections between them are strictly narrow beam only. So the southern (green), East Anglian (red), northern (blue) and western (red) widebeam waterways all remain separate from each other – at least for the forseeable future. The Midland and north western narrow canals are shown in black

And though the connected inland system is a principal attraction of Britain's waterways there are some important unconnected water systems that attract sizeable numbers of owners and holidaymakers. Chief among these are the Norfolk and Suffolk Broads where holiday boating has flourished longer than anywhere else in Britain.

This network of lakes and rivers, augmented by the flooded relics of medieval peat cuttings offers easy, lock-free cruising in the distinctive East Anglian landscape, predominantly rural and rich in wildlife. Though some sections of the Broads can get very busy in high summer, there are many smaller rivers and creeks to discover off the beaten track.

The Broads supports many hire-boat fleets. Many holiday-makers return year after year, and there are few boaters who have never spent at least one holiday afloat in Broadland. Conversely, the Broads have fewer private boat-owners than the main waterway system.

Scotland has two great coast-to-coast canals. The Forth & Clyde Canal, crossing the Scottish lowlands from Grangemouth to Glasgow, re-opened in 2001, together with a connecting canal to Edinburgh (the Union Canal). The two are linked by the stunning rotating boat lift, the Falkirk Wheel – a trip to which is enough on its own to make a holiday here worthwhile.

Further north, the Caledonian Canal follows the Great Glen, Scotland's great fault-line, from Fort William to Inverness. This marvellously spectacular route comprises short canal sections linking natural lochs – of which Loch Ness is one. Boats are available for hire on both the Caledonian and the Forth & Clyde, which have small, though growing, numbers of private boats.

Finally one must not forget the scenic lakes of the English Lake District, many of which have their own resident boating populations of power and sailing craft as well as being popular trailboat destinations. At one time lakes like Windemere and Coniston had no speed limits and were famous for their powerboat racing but a speed limit has put an end to this.

Boating is greatly enjoyable in itself, but the inland waterways' unique appeal comes just as much from what you'll find on the waterside. Britain's canals and rivers are lined with pubs and restaurants, quiet country villages, wildlife sites, museums, and countless more attractions. Discovering life on the other side of the towpath is one of the things that sets inland cruising apart from offshore boating.

The canals were built to serve industry as these canalside kiln in the Potteries reminds us

Now restored to working glory, the Anderton Boat Lift is well worth a trip

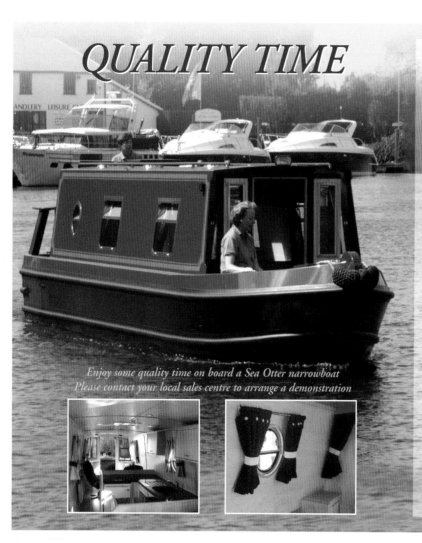
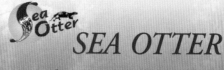

What sort of Boat?

There's a boat to suit just about every pocket and every lifestyle, from secondhand weekend glass-fibre cruiser to luxurious, purpose designed narrowboat

The working narrow boat had a rear boatman's cabin living quarters and a large, load carrying hold. This survivor now sells rope fenders and canalware

Small day boats like this, either outboard or even electric powered offer an easy route afloat

The modern narrowboat has evolved from the working canal boats of the past into a very different purpose-designed holiday or live-aboard craft

Glass-fibre cruisers are very popular river boats and can be found in all shapes, sizes and prices

T he inland waterways are a great democracy. Sharing a busy lock you'll likely find a £¼ million Dutch barge, ageing glass-fibre cruiser, holiday hire narrowboat and immaculate replica working boat. So whether you have £250 or £250,000 to spend, somewhere there is a boat for you.

GLASS FIBRE CRUISERS

This catch-all name embraces everything from tiny two-seaters with outboard engines to vast flying-bridge luxury craft capable of coastal as well as river use. As grp hulls are formed in moulds boats can be designed with complex shapes but the cost of these moulds means that they are made in series-production rather than as one-offs.

A small secondhand grp river cruiser is a good way to tip a toe into boat ownership: boats can be found for relatively small sums and if bought carefully will hold their value well. Since marina charges and licence fees are length related, running costs are relatively low too.

A 20ft cruiser will typically offer reasonably good 2+2 accommodation, a practical galley and toilet. It will also be responsive and easy for the beginner to handle – and even on crowded riversides there is often somewhere for a little 20 footer to sneak in and moor up!

The classified columns of boating magazines are full of adverts for small used grp cruisers: Freeman, Seamaster, Elysian and Viking are all popular makes, offering boats in mid-20 feet lengths with typically two-plus-two accommodation and either diesel or petrol power. Freeman, in particular, has always been highly regarded as a very traditional small boat with smart chrome fittings and plenty of veneered woodwork inside. As we have said, though, only a few narrow beam 'canal cruisers' can use the narrow canals.

Glass-fibre boats are surprisingly tough – and have the advantage of not needing painting. It has to be remembered, though, that many of these small craft are 30 or more years old. Older grp hulls can show signs of osmosis – a blistering deterioration of the glass-fibre underwater which can be difficult and expensive to cure – and many boats are often victims of tinkering owners with varying degrees of DIY skills!

Relatively few companies build small plastic river cruisers today: among them are Viking which is still building boats with a range of 20 – 26ft craft and Dolphin, which recently introduced a new range of 16–22ft boats.

Larger and more powerful cruisers are popular on our bigger rivers; some can also happily do estuary and even cross-Channel trips. Glass fibre (in osmosis resistant forms these days) is still the most popular construction medium though higher up the price range steel and aluminium are also widely used for hulls.

NARROWBOATS

The narrowboat has become the vessel of choice for many inland waterway users. It provides 'go anywhere' proportions – and even weekend boaters like to dream of continuously cruising the inland network – as well as offering all the comforts of home, including often quite literally the kitchen sink and a washing machine!

The narrowboat evolved to suit our narrow canals, where not just width but height under low, tight bridges and shallow water depths are design constraints. As a slow-moving, predominantly still-water craft it also doesn't need the complex vee-hull shapes of faster river and coastal boats.

This money-no-object narrowboat Northwich tug replica with its Gardner 2L2 engine could be called the Rolls-Royce of the canals

Instead, the hull is flat-bottomed and, generally, straight sided. On this is set an almost full-length cabin. In the 1970s this was regularly made from glass-fibre but steel is now universally used throughout.

The result is a relatively simple, 'box' structure that can be formed from sheet steel with the minimum of folding and pressing, which helps keep manufacturing costs down. It has also enabled narrowboat shell building to become something of a cottage industry, with small builders adding individual touches of style and detail to the basic shape. We will look in more detail at hull design and options on page 54.

Narrowboats can be found in all sizes, from as short as 20ft right up to the 70ft maximum capable of fitting the system's locks. Older boats tended to be at the shorter end of the spectrum but today's more affluent buyers prefer the greater space of boats around 55-60ft.

The narrowness of the boat dictates its interior layout, with one 'room' following the next. Nevertheless, boat fitters have used remarkable imagination to come up with a wide variety of interior layouts as we shall see later.

While most narrowboats are now of the 'floating home' style, there are variations. Former working boats have been converted to leisure use, with accommodation under the load carrying 'cloths' of the hold, while the 'replica' working boat with vintage engine displayed to view in an engine room and elaborately painted boatman's cabin is an enthusiast favourite. Replicas of the elegant inspection launches are less common.

Not quite all narrowboats are made in steel. Sea Otter pioneered aluminium construction for small, trailable craft which also cleverly used disposable water ballast to reduce weight when towing. These days they build narrowboats of every size as well as Dutch barges in marine grade aluminium, a material which, as the company likes to point out, is far more resistant to corrosion than steel and needs much less frequent hull 'blacking' and painting than the steel boat which needs to be taken out of the water for blacking at least every two years.

DUTCH BARGES

There's no denying that, however well planned, the narrowboat is restricted in space. For that reason an increasing number of buyers looking for a residential boat or for something capable of longer term cruising – in Europe as well as the UK – are opting for the Dutch barge.

The name 'Dutch barge' covers a much wider spectrum of boats than the narrowboat. The 'luxemotor'-style is the best known and arguably best looking, with a curvaceous hull and central or rear wheelhouse (collapsible for passing under low bridges). It is the style on which leisure barge builders base their craft. The 'tjalk' has a more rounded bow, reflecting its origins as a sailing barge.

Most have a vee-section hull and can be suitable for estuary work, or even to cross the North Sea in calm weather, but they are inland not sea-going vessels.

Dutch barges range from former cargo boats, converted to residential use on budgets that go from shoestring to lottery winning, through to plush purpose designed leisure boats. And in size from 40ft long 'mini barges' up to 100ft plus leviathans. Widths range from 10ft to 14ft plus so they provide much more space than the narrow canal craft.

Former working barges appear to last well and riveted iron hull boats as much as 100 years old are not uncommon in the classified columns. Unconverted examples to be found for sale in Europe potentially offer 'a lot of boat for the money' as the hold space can be converted to residential use but they do need to be bought with very great care!

A lower cost alternative to the Dutch barge is the 'widebeam' – a broaded version of the narrowboat. Lacking something in exterior aesthetics perhaps, it does offer considerable space inside for residential or long-term boaters. Another rather different 'mongrel' design is the narrowbeam Dutch barge, attractively barge-like in profile and layout but narrow enough to traverse the narrow canals.

This widebeam might not have the visual style of a Dutch barge but its spacious interior makes it an ideal live-aboard, offering a double and two single cabins

Not every narrowboat need be expensive: this tidy condition little 26ft ex-hire boat was on sale for under £10,000 recently

Too wide for the narrow canals but otherwise the elegant and roomy Dutch barge is ideal for exploring the waterways in both Britain and Europe

12 *THE CANAL BOAT MANUAL*

Rules and Regulations

Two important sets of regulations govern most of the powered craft on our inland waterway system

THE RECREATIONAL CRAFT DIRECTIVE

The RCD is the most important regulation governing modern pleasure boats. It is an EC Directive applicable throughout the EU and EEA (European Economic Area) and is designed to protect boat buyers and users, as well as to enable freedom of movement of goods.

It has applied since June 1998 to all boats between 2.5 and 24 metres long with a few exceptions such as canoes, racing boats or hovercraft. It covers all essential aspects of a boat's design and construction, with the emphasis on safety.

On January 1, 2007 the last phase of a new Amending Directive came into effect which extends its scope to include limiting boat and engine noise and exhaust emissions as well as updating some of the original regulations.

The engine changes only apply to new boats and engines: existing engines can continue to be used but replacement ones must comply. A used boat can also now be imported from outside the EU using new 'Post Construction Assessment' rules.

The RCD is enforced in the UK by Trading Standards. It is essential that anyone buying a new boat or a used boat that was not already in use in the EC/EEA on June 16, 1998, or importing a boat from outside the EU, should understand the requirements of the RCD. If a boat does not comply it may be impossible to use, insure or sell. They may also be asked to make it comply. They need to look out for five things on the boat:

- A builder's plate: this has the maker's details and technical information including the design category (see below) and maximum loading weight.
- A CE mark, carried on the builder's plate.
- A Craft or Hull Identification Number, (CIN or HIN): this unique number identifies builder, country and date of build. It is carried in two places on the boat, one of them hidden as a security check.
- An owner's manual with the information needed to use and maintain the boat safely.
- A declaration of conformity (found in the manual). It is illegal to sell an eligible craft without this.

Most canal boats are in design category 'D', meaning they are built to suit inland waterway use rather than more demanding open water conditions. They can therefore be 'self certified' for compliance by the builder – and this is what will happen if you buy a fully completed boat.

SAILAWAYS AND SELF-BUILDS

There are special requirements for individuals completing a hull or a sailaway. They should receive an Annex IIIa declaration from the hull builder or sailaway supplier which states that it meets the essential requirements of the RCD up to the point at which it has been built.

When the boat is finally completed, the last person in the chain (the self-builder in this case) is officially termed the manufacturer and must ensure that the completed craft complies with the RCD. They are responsible for applying the CE mark and producing an owner's manual. An immediate benefit of CE marking the craft is that a Boat Safety Scheme Certificate can be applied for without inspection.

An eligible boat can only be exempt from RCD requirements if it is classed as a 'home build'. This means it is built from scratch or from a sailaway by a private individual who must then keep it for their own personal, private use and not offer it for sale for five years. (The five year period starts from when the boat is first used on the water.)

Remember that it will still need a BSS certificate for licensing so BSS safety requirements must be complied with. We always advise a DIY builder to seek advice from a surveyor experienced in RCD and BSS compliance to avoid potential problems.

Anyone buying a home-build boat secondhand must ask for adequate proof of the five year ownership period, including BSS certificates, waterway licences, mooring invoices etc.

OTHER BOATS

Any secondhand commercial craft, or any other exempt craft, being bought with a view to conversion for recreational use, will have to comply with the RCD and to do so will need to undergo a Post Construction Assessment (PCA).

A new or secondhand boat imported from outside the EC, and not CE marked, must be shown to comply with the regulations by undertaking a PCA.

An official 'Notified Body', who will carry out the assessment and deal with the technical and compliance formalities must then be employed. There are four in the UK – details on the DTI website.

This builder's plate is very prominently displayed

BOAT SAFETY SCHEME

The Boat Safety Scheme (BSS), sometimes called the MoT test for boats, was set up by British Waterways and the Environment Agency in 1997 as a set of safety standards for inland waterway craft. After some delay the scheme will now be extended to the Broads where it will be phased in from April 2007.

All boats on these inland waterways must have a valid BSS certificate in order to be eligible for their annual navigation licence. The certificate is issued after inspection by an approved BSS examiner and lasts for four years.

The BSS requirements cover safety, environmental and best safety practice across all major areas of the boat – engine, electrical, LPG gas, fire safety, ventilation and so on. They are divided into two categories: Mandatory and Advisory.

Mandatory items are those that British Waterways and the Environment Agency insist a privately-owned boat must comply with as they are either essential safety or anti-pollution measures.

Advisory Check List items concern to best safety practice issues. Although a privately-owned boat does not have to comply with these items to get a BSS certificate it is strongly recommended by the BSS that you do.

It has to be stressed that a BSS certificate is only an indicator of the state of safety of the boat at the time it was tested – the buyer of a used boat should take particular care that safety features are still up to scratch. Nor is a BSS certificate a substitute for a full survey when buying a boat – it looks at safety and environmental issues, not structural ones, such as engine or hull condition.

MORE INFORMATION

Further information on the RCD is available from the Department of Trade and Industry **www.dti.gov.uk/innovation/strd/ecdirect/ page12637.html**, and the RYA **www.rya.org.uk/knowledgebase/technical/ reccraftdir.html**

The RYA and British Marine Federation run an RCD document download site **www.rcdweb.com** and Hampshire County Council's website has comprehensive plain language information at **www.hants.gov.uk** (search using 'RCD'), including a section for canal boats.

Detailed information about the Boat Safety Scheme can be found on the BSS website, **www.boatsafetyscheme.com** where the full BSS booklet can also be downloaded.

Buying a new boat

A new narrowboat is a big investment and buying one is something that should be done with some care

Boats – like suits – come in two ways: off-the-peg or made-to-measure. Smaller boats, including most of the popular glass-fibre cruisers, are sold with standard specifications that can be augmented by a limited number of options. A bit like choosing the seat trim or the grade of stereo on your new Ford Focus hatchback.

A sizeable minority of narrowboats can also be bought off-the-peg but are generally offered with a much wider range of options and extras. You can, as it were, choose estate car or convertible as well as engine size and interior trim if they are on the manufacturer's list but you can't ask for wire wheels or a pink leather trim if they aren't.

Most canal boats, on the other hand, are bespoke-built to their owner's requirements. And if you want the canalboating equivalent of wire wheels or pink leather, you can have it – the only proviso being that it fits in with the appropriate rules and regulations.

Buying a new narrowboat represents a very substantial financial investment but it is surprising how many people take such a big step with little forethought. They will sell up their home or take on a substantial marine mortgage with scarcely a consideration for the consequences.

Fortunately, in the great majority of cases, things go very well and the only consequences are good ones – but in a minority of cases there are problems and, in the worst cases people end up losing large

Gather information from plenty of different companies to help you with your planning and researches

The Crick Boat Show is the year's big event for anyone thinking of buying a narrowboat with 40 or more new boats to examine in detail

Before you buy, make sure you take a close look at different styles and layouts, and discuss your ideas with the boatbuilders

amounts of money. Buying a new canal boat then, is something that should be entered into carefully.

So where to start? The first step is to do your research. You may be convinced that the boating life is for you but before splashing out, do some fundamental research. Stroll along the towpaths, talk to other boat owners – they are friendly and invariably very willing to share their experiences – visit marinas, hire a boat, preferably several times and out of season.

Don't just treat it as a holiday but as a fact finding expedition to work out all the things you enjoy, dislike, cannot live without and of course can do without. An idea of what you want from a boat should be starting to form in your mind.

Visit boat shows such as the Crick Show or IWA National Festival where you can view new boats close up so you can compare builders – and their prices. New narrowboats can be bought from under £40,000 to over £100,000. At 2006 prices, around £1000 per foot length of boat is about the bare minimum for an off-the-peg narrowboat. A state-of-the-art custom boat will cost double that! At the moment a good-quality, well-equipped mid-range custom boat will be around £1400 a foot.

You need to draw up your key requirements at an early stage and bear in mind that the more often you change your mind during the build process, the more delayed your finished boat is likely to be (and the more expensive!) Even a standard boat will be available with a large number of extra cost features and it's important to get the ones you need. Don't waste your money on options you won't need but, equally, don't skimp – if you are intending to live aboard, for example, you will need good heating and heavy duty electrical systems.

Next step is to draw up a short-list of potential builders and visit them at their yards. Ask to see previous fit-outs that are on the water and talk to their owners. Visit the hull builder, too. They can offer minor style variations that might just suit you better than the standard yard specification.

If you are having an expensive custom boat

built, recognise that you, the builder and his team are going to spend a good deal of time together so be very sure you gel together; if in doubt look elsewhere.

FINANCING YOUR BOAT

Some people are lucky enough to finance their purchase through the sale of a house or maturation of an insurance policy but others will need some sort of loan. Many banks and finance houses now offer 'marine mortgages' which are, effectively, loans secured on the value of the boat. Typically these can be for up to 80 per cent of the boat's cost and repayable for up to ten years.

The title of the boat will need to be registered and you will be responsible for paying off the loan if the boat is sold.

BUYING SAFELY

Boat builders do build some craft on spec for use at boat shows and such like but most of their output – even the off-the-shelf boats – will be built to order and they will expect their customers to pay for their new boat in stages as it is being built. This shares the financial load (and risk) between builder and customer.

For this reason the most important form of protection for both sides is a correctly drawn up contract. This will transfer ownership of the boat in stages to the customer as monies are paid over.

The British Marine Federation (BMF) provides a standard stage payments contract which its members should use. This was drawn up after consultations between the Royal Yachting Association (RYA) overseeing the interests of consumers and the BMF representing the industry. As such it has become a well established boating industry standard.

Many canal boat builders are BMF members (and members of its subsidiary organisation the Canal Boatbuilders Association, the CBA). Other builders who are not members generally use the BMF contract as well.

If you are buying a new boat you should insist that a BMF contract is used or, if the builder offers an alternative version you should ask your solicitor to check it carefully.

The contract is extremely comprehensive: it will detail specification, price, delivery date, and provision of a pre-delivery inspection and trial as well as the payment structure. The more carefully the contract is drawn up, the less cause there will be for problems during the build – on either side.

It is particularly important for the boat's specification to be itemised in detail: for example is signwriting included, are ropes, pins, poles, boathook

Builder's plate with CE mark shows RCD compliance

Custom builders will build what you want but most have a house style. Above is a Wharf House interior. Left from top, Braidbar, Soar Valley, Fernwood

and an anchor provided, how many gas bottles are there, is the water tank stainless steel or integral, what about curtains, are there any costs for craneage in of the finished boat etc etc? All small points but the cost soon adds up.

An agreed delivery date is also included in the contract and the builder is only allowed to extend this because of 'force majeure' – flood, fire etc. Despite this, late delivery remains a common cause of complaint by buyers. If you have a crucial delivery deadline, such as the sale of a house, put this in the contract. It is worth pointing out, though, that many delays are caused by customers making frequent changes to the boat while work is in progress. The BMF contract in fact specifies that changes and their effect on timing and price have to be agreed in writing by both parties.

The payment and ownership structure is at the heart of the contract. The timing and size of stage payments is a matter for agreement between you and your builder but do not be persuaded into handing over large sums in advance of work done – if in any doubt ask the advice of a surveyor or simply talk to other boatbuilders.

A typical payment structure would be:

* An initial, usually non-refundable payment on signing of the contract. This can be as little as £1000 but should not be more than ten per cent of the total price.
* On completion of the shell, at which point ownership of the shell passes to the customer.
* On installation of the engine. Again with ownership passing to the customer.
* On completion of the fit-out.
* A final balance, of around five to ten per cent to be paid on hand-over after a successful inspection and trial.

In the BMF contract, ownership of equipment passes to the customer as it is bought for the boat. Should a boatbuilder run into difficulties and go into administration, problems can arise for the customer for two reasons. Either equipment bought for a specific boat cannot be identified and is therefore liable to be sold to pay off debts (with the Inland

The Polish-built Aqualine Manhattan shows that impressive quality is available in an 'off-the-peg' boat

Revenue and VAT taking first claim) or the builder has failed to pay his customers' money to his suppliers – using it to prop up his struggling business instead – and hence the equipment's ownership remains with its supplier. That could be a £25 pump or your £25,000 shell!

These things happen rarely but they do happen so it is as well to take precautions. Ensure that significant items you have paid for are marked as being for your boat; ask for and record the serial number of your engine and so on. You might also feel that you would like to pay major suppliers such as engine and shell builders direct.

Most importantly, keep in touch with your builder and visit regularly during the build. The professional builder will welcome visits. This way you will be able to monitor progress on your boat and resolve any queries or problems before it's too late. Keep notes of any changes that you and the builder agree during a visit and confirm them later in writing. Take plenty of photographs of the work

being done on your boat – they will be a fascinating record to look back on and useful if there are problems. Remember that successfully building a boat is a two-way process: try not to be a difficult customer with constant changes of mind, late payments and unreasonable demands.

If you can't make regular visits yourself it is a good idea to appoint a surveyor to supervise the build for you. He can make sure that the build is progressing properly and also that the boat conforms to the Recreational Craft Directive (RCD) – see separate panel. You may baulk at the extra cost but if it points up problems, it could be money well spent.

All this might seem to be a gloomy picture of the relationship between builder and customer. It isn't meant to be: the great majority of new boats are the result of a happy and fruitful working relationship. Sadly, problems when they do arise can be big ones and make headlines. Make sure they don't happen to you and that you join the ranks of happy boat owners.

Be sure to visit your builder regularly during construction and fit-out

SHARED OWNERSHIP

Buying and running a canal boat is expensive but so too is hiring one for regular holiday trips. As a result, shared ownership schemes have become very popular as a half-way house.

Shared ownership schemes do exactly what it says on the tin: a group or 'syndicate' share the ownership of the boat, buying a certain number of annual weeks usage as their 'share'.

They can be as simple as an unofficial group of friends banding together to buy and run a used boat, but a number of companies now operate extremely sophisticated schemes that build boats, co-ordinate sharing, manage the boats, buy and sell shares and take care of maintenance. Names like Ownerships, Challenger and Carefree Cruising are all well known.

The boats themselves are generally built to similar levels of quality and equipment as good quality private craft, rather than the sometimes rather functional layouts of hire boats.

The schemes should not be confused with timeshare operations (of which there are several) that offer purchase of a fixed period each year for a finite number of years.

Under the various share schemes, syndicate members own their portion of their particular boat, can sell their share in it freely and can choose different holiday periods each year.

The various schemes differ greatly in detail – some have what appear to be extremely complex arrangements of distributing weeks designed to create fair sharing of holiday periods while others have more informal set-ups that rely on shareholders swapping weeks between themselves. Different schemes will suit different customers.

If you worry that you are sharing ownership with people who may smoke, bring a smelly dog on board or not clean up as well as they should, schemes report that sharers generally are a considerate group who will leave boats scrupulously clean at the end of their holidays. (Some companies have 'no smoking' and 'no pets' boats, too.)

Depending on the scheme and choice of weeks a one-twelfth (four week) ownership share in a boat might cost between £7000 and £10,000 plus an annual contribution towards mooring, maintenance and so on.

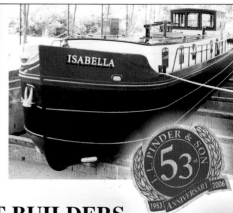

Sailaways

As the costs of fully fitted narrowboats go up, sailaways have become an increasingly popular option but just how easy is it to turn that dark bare shell into a floating palace?

FROM THIS...

T o build a narrowboat from scratch, including the steelwork, is beyond most people. However, fitting out a shell could be the answer for many DIY enthusiasts, providing that they really do have the skills needed and are aware of what needs to be done and how long it can take.

The increasingly popular 'sailaway' can be cheaper than buying a ready-made boat, but you will have to be serious about the amount of time and effort needed to produce a decent boat that you (and future owners) will be proud of.

WHERE DO I START?

A BASIC SHELL
This is the minimum: the hull and superstructure, most often with a 10mm baseplate, 6 or 8mm hull sides and a 3 or 4mm cabin top. Internal steel framing gives the shell rigidity and allows timber

battens to be attached to take the lining materials. The engine beds, weed hatch and drip tray will be in place, along with the diesel tank (usually around 40 gallons) in the stern. The rudder, tiller and bearings are fitted, although the stern tube is probably only a drilled hole or threaded boss.

Window apertures may or may not be cut, depending on you and your builder. The fresh water tank might be integral with the shell.

Other items that should be included are handrails, gas locker, mooring studs/cleats, fender points, engine room/space bulkhead. The hull will be painted in blacking and the superstructure in primer. The inside will be in basic primer or red oxide.

SHELL AND ENGINE
A professional engine installation means that the boat is ready to move, although the electrics are usually very basic and may just consist of the engine starter

battery. The boat may be moveable but rain water will get inside and the lack of ballast will make it very difficult to cruise any distance.

WATERTIGHT SAILAWAY
This is a moveable shell, where windows/portholes and doors are fitted so the boat is secure and moveable – although the same ballast problems are present. Having the builder fit windows and doors usually means a neater job: fitting windows can be difficult and cutting steel is certainly not easy!

SAILAWAY SHELL
The typical "sailaway" has basic ballast and flooring fitted – although it needs to be able to be lifted so final trimming material can be added. This at least gives the basis of having somewhere to work as you fit out.

Many shell builders offer spray-foam insulation which, if applied carefully, is excellent as long as it is trimmed back. Often timber battens are attached to the shell framing to make it easier to fit the lining material.

A fully lined sailaway will have all insulation, lining and trims in place. Some builders will also fit a number of basic bulkheads, to allow a head start. Having the lining in place means that the wiring for appliances (especially lights) must have been in place, or conduit fitted (with draw-wires) to allow wiring to be added later.

Some companies offer further levels of fitting, including calorifiers, central heating systems, plumbing, electrical systems and so on, fitted all ready to use.

A point worth remembering, though, is that the basic lining out of the boat is one of the easier (if time-consuming) fitting-out carpentry jobs – it's the finishing joinery that demands real skill. So don't waste precious budget on work you could do yourself.

PART-FIT
This could include the galley and bathroom fitted, ready to use, so the boat can be "camped" on while the rest of the boat is finished. The level of fit out is only as limited as the depth of your budget.

THE SKILLS NEEDED
How good are you with woodwork? Fitting a boat is not really just making simple shapes. You need to be proficient with hand and electric tools. You will also need a lot of tools: cheap DIY ones are not really strong enough for the job. Knowing how to use them is another matter! It is not worth trying to bodge the job in hand.

Lining a boat, as we said, is the easier bit, however, once the bulkheads are fitted the more tricky parts start. Fitting the galley is not really a matter of nipping to the local DIY centre and buying ready-to-assemble kitchen units. They probably won't fit without work, and may be made of MDF, which can absorb water quite quickly, becoming ruined in a matter of months, as they swell in the damp atmosphere of your unfinished boat.

Building the toilet compartment is the only other main part, other than the galley, which needs to be done before the boat is cruiseable. The rest of the boat can 'make-do' with free-standing furniture, until such time as you want to tackle them – which for many amateur fitters is still a distant prospect.

How good is your knowledge of electrical systems? Do you know about combating voltage

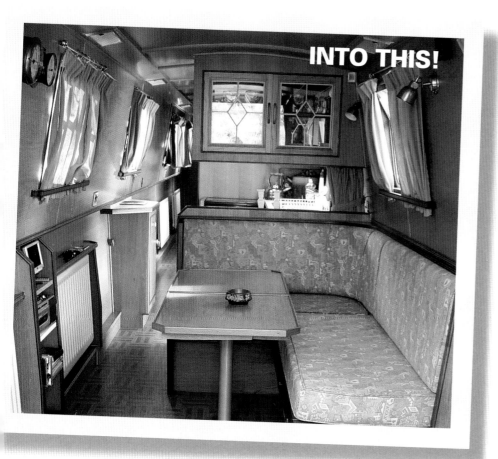

INTO THIS!

drop, for example? If the answer is "not sure" then you will need to brush up on your background information before planning. Although 12V DC systems are not inherently dangerous (unlikely to kill you), poorly fitted systems can short circuit, causing corrosion or, more seriously, overheating and potential fires. 'Mains' electric (230V AC) on the other hand, can kill. Unless you are very sure of your competence, don't go near it. Take advice or preferably get a marine electrician to do the job. Water, steel and 230V are a potentially lethal combination.

Gas systems (usually propane) are not for the amateur. All work on gas pipework, including connecting appliances, must be done by an approved CORGI (council of registered gas installers) fitter. They must also be qualified in LPG systems for use on marine craft, as different standards apply to household installations.

Basic plumbing is not usually difficult on a boat, provided that you use plastic push-fit type pipes and fittings and have planned thoroughly in advance!

External painting to a basic finish is usually within most boaters' grasp, and very good results can be obtained with patience. Signwriting is something that should really be left to a professional, as if it is poorly-executed, it can ruin the exterior of an otherwise fine craft!

At 24, Chris Morrison decided to tackle the ultimate self-build – from a bare Reeves shell upwards, including painting and even marinising his engine

"My boat is more of a floataway as I even installed the engine myself (hence the name *Drift-A-Way*)

I have done a fair bit of work with cars in the past so dealing with the engine installation wasn't a problem.

I work in electronics so the electrics were no problem. Plumbing isn't a big deal and some quick research on the internet got me up to speed on what is the norm for a narrowboat. I'm aiming for a gas-free boat so dealing with gas regulations hasn't been an issue.

Carpentry is my weak point: it has been a fairly steep learning curve. Also I underestimated how difficult a good paint job would be. I've spray-painted car parts before but marine paints are a different story altogether.

The most difficult part has been understanding the requirements of the Recreational Craft Directive with what is required and when. I had a Boat Safety Scheme test in March to allow me to re-license the boat. The shell was completed in April 2005 and this time next year is the target for completion but I don't think it will ever be finished 100 per cent, I'll always be tweaking.

I'm only able to work evenings and every other weekend so I'm looking at just over two years start to finish but there is no hurry."

His Top Tips

1 Don't underestimate the cost of all the odds and sods – e.g. a water pump is around £90 then you'll need the strainer at £12 and BSP-to-push-fit pipe adaptors etc.
2 Always do your homework before committing to anything.
3 Don't underestimate the cost of tools. Budget for LOTS of drill bits.
4 Don't underestimate how long it takes to get things done – be it painting or cutting holes in steel. (Drilling hundreds of holes in steel above your head is hard work!
5 Factor in potential price rises on parts. For example in 12 months I've seen brass skin fittings increase by 50%.
6 Always screw not glue or nail where possible. Not being able to get things apart again can be frustrating – cut floorboards so that some can still be removed when the boat is complete.
7 Always use stainless steel screws even though they are ten times the cost of ordinary screws (which can rust through in just one winter).
8 I could go on and on...
Follow Chris's progress at www.aopu10.dsl.pipex.com/ boatpages

Keep warm while you work

Not much room to work inside

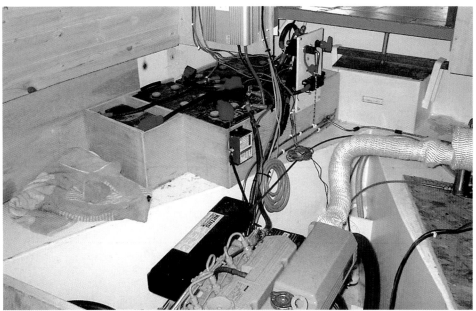

You need to know what you are doing before tackling major installation tasks

Richard and Sue Attwood fitted out their 58ft semi-trad Colecraft sailaway, *Windor* using many conventional 'land' fittings

We started with a fully lined sailaway and only had domestic DIY skills. As well as installing the fixtures and fittings, we also did all the DC and AC wiring and plumbing. Central heating will be fitted later in the year.

Their Top Tips

1 I would say to anyone wanting to do a fitout – spend time planning the fitout and research what is available on the domestic DIY market eg. B&Q, IKEA, Focus etc.

2 We used a four foot domestic bed, an IKEA sink unit in the bathroom and a B&Q shower tray and door. All the kitchen units came from B&Q and were no problem to fit. The floor is covered with IKEA laminate flooring and the two chairs are from Focus. The saloon wall light is from IKEA and the stove is a Hunter Hawk.

3 The fridge is a normal 240V domestic unit. The sink is a stainless steel domestic unit with domestic taps. Dining is at a normal kitchen table – of the correct size. We spotted one on a private boat for sale at Braunston Marina.

4 Finally, don't be afraid to ask advice from other boaters, Google waterways newsgroup and the World Canal Forum.

IKEA basin unit and B&Q kitchen units.

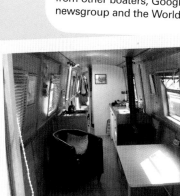

The impressive end results

Remember that the finished boat will be sold at some point so the quality of the final fit out is very important. Many professionally-lined sailaways are then fitted out with poor joinery skills; rough edges, ill-fitting trims and so on. It is not unknown for boats to end up less in value than the sum of their parts. Bear in mind that future buyers can be very picky about craft and that surveyors can find even the smallest fault in a pre-purchase inspection.

WHERE CAN YOU WORK?

A mooring at the bottom of a garden would be the ideal for convenience. Remembering that fitting a boat will probably take all of your spare time, holiday allowance and quite a few evenings for two years or more, you do not want to spend hours travelling to the boat to work on it.

The mooring is going to need easy access for unloading large and heavy goods from a car. A shore-side 230V supply is useful – a generator may become noisy (to others) and expensive to run.

Trying to fit a boat while cruising just prolongs the process and can really distract others if you turn the towpath into part of your workshop, scattering wood, tools and waste alongside your boat. Plus, by the time you finish the fitting, some parts of the boat will look decidedly well-used!

WHAT SHOULD I LOOK FOR?

A boat is only as good as the shell it is based on. A high-quality fit out in a budget shell will be worth far less than an upmarket craft with a basic interior. You can always alter or even refit the interior, but you can't improve the shell. The more detailed, curvy and well-built hulls usually handle well and look much better.

There are some items that are particularly worth thinking about when buying the shell – they may increase value and convenience in the future.

Water tanks that are integral with the shell are cheaper but need special painting every few years. They can be a source of corrosion, and the access hatch often leaks, allowing all sort of unsavoury things into the tank! Separate tanks, of stainless steel, are usually more popular, although often smaller.

Holding tanks for pump-out toilets integral with the shell were once popular but are probably not such a good idea as they cannot be easily removed (should you or a future owner want to change the toilet system).

The majority of the outside parts of the boat should be fabricated of steel and the steel doors and hatches are much more secure than wooden ones.

Pole and plank holders are useful, as are centre mooring studs/rings. Engine access covers are better made of something lighter as steel sheet is hard to lift!

A bow thruster tube could be fitted even if you do not actually plan fitting a thruster at the moment. One might be useful in the future, although the tube is a potential corrosion trap as it is hard to paint inside.

If buying lined or part-lined ensure that an anti-corrosive treatment, such as Waxoyl, is applied before the ballast is laid. There also needs to be ventilation under the floor, from fore-to-aft, to reduce condensation build-up.

Many boaters take the craft in primer and leave it like that for the few years it takes to fit. Primer is not really waterproof: it is to provide a base for the other layers of paint. However, look at many young craft being fitted out and there are plenty of signs of

Cheap but not always very cheerful – a low cost covered dock

corrosion. A good bet would be to specify the hull to be grit blasted (to SA2.5 standard), and a two-pack epoxy paint to be applied to the hull below the waterline.

The grit blasting removes any mill scale formed during the steel rolling process. Left on the steel, it ends up increasing in volume after a few years, taking much of the paint covering with it.

Grit blasting is messy but future buyers will be thankful of it. The expensive two-pack coating will not need repainting for a lot longer than basic bitumen based ones.

The superstructure should receive at least one coat of undercoat and two of top gloss to help prevent corrosion. By the time the craft is finished, this can be rubbed down and a fancy paint scheme applied. In the meantime, the basic finish will protect your investment.

Also, ensure that magnesium anodes of the correct size are present from the start and that they are low enough to be submerged while the boat is being fitted out.

This will reduce the chance of corrosion even further as the magnesium will react instead of the steel.

PLAN, PLAN AND PLAN AGAIN
When ordering a sailaway, make sure you have finalised your plans and had them checked by someone! Then check again. And again.

For example, once window apertures have been cut they cannot be altered! A bulkhead across a window shows a future buyer that someone didn't think!

Hull outlets for sinks and showers are not easy to cut yourself, so you need to specify exactly where they must go. It might be worth fitting vents and chimney collars after the bulk of the lining is fitted, or at least until you are sure that everything is going to plan.

THE RULES
All new boats need a declaration of conformity to the Recreation Craft Directive (RCD). A new hull or sailaway will come with one.

However, the builder of a new craft – that means you – is responsible for the documentation (which is quite considerable) and marking of the

Matt Allard started his build of Nb *Kathlyn* with a lined-out sailaway from the New Boat Company

Smart outside but work goes on

"Before I started to fit out my sailaway my only experience was doing DIY at home. I had never owned or fitted out another boat and really did not know what to expect, but I found as long as you have a good grounding in DIY and are willing to give most things a try then nothing will be too challenging.

Obviously you leave anything to do with the gas install and preferably the 240V install to the experts, but other than that, everything is fairly safe stuff.

I personally also got someone from the boat company to install all the skin fittings (sink and shower outlets) as the thought of drilling holes in the outside of my watertight boat filled me with a bit of fear. After seeing the size of drill

bits he needed to cut the holes I think it was money well spent.

I am still only part way through the fit-out of my boat but I have already learnt a lot.

www.kathlyn.co.uk

His Top Tips
1 Order a copy of the Boat Safety Scheme book from www.boatsafetyscheme.com. It is free and gives all the information you need to know about keeping the boat safe and in compliance with the BSS. It will keep you on the straight and narrow.

2 Talk to lots of people and ask their advice. There is bound to be someone nearby who has fitted their boat out and it is always reassuring that what you have thought of doing is a good idea. Don't be afraid though to try something new, it is what will make your boat unique.

3 Look at as many show boats as possible and take pictures of the bits you like. If you can, measure them up as well: it will help you with space layout in your boat.

4 Get insurance that covers your boat for its increasing value over the year specifically written for fitting out a boat. Also make sure it covers your tools on board.

5 Remember the size of your doors, they are not as big as in a house and the rear doors maybe smaller than you think. Not everything will fit through them and a sheet of 8x4in wood may only go in the front doors.

6 Most of all enjoy fitting it out, the enjoyment of the fit-out is probably one of the reasons you choose to do it yourself.

Building the bed frame

How it all started – the sailaway from New Boat Company

craft when it is completed.

Fortunately, if you keep your craft for five years after it has been completed (which is a moot point – when is a self-fitted boat actually finished?) before selling it, you can avoid the paperwork.

But don't rely on this – your circumstances may change and you may sell early. If in any doubt, speak to an advisor!

All boats over four years old need to have a

Boat Safety Certificate, if on most of Britain's waterway network. It is worth getting one from the start. Employ a local surveyor to inspect the boat at regular intervals – such as after installation of main systems, half-way through the fit, and so on. A good surveyor will be able to help you with RCD compliance too.

If you stick to the advice in the Boat Safety Guide, plus a healthy dose of common sense, then

Wiring needn't be hard but you must be careful on cable sizes and voltage drop

you should be OK. If you are in any doubt, a surveyor or boat safety scheme examiner will be able to help you out.

Do not forget that you will need insurance for the craft, especially if it is afloat. Some insurance companies offer staged protection, with the value of the cover increasing as the work progresses.

Safety while fitting out is obvious, but aside from personal injury (a good knowledge of first aid, a stocked kit and preferably not working alone), fires are not uncommon while cutting, drilling, etc. Make sure you tidy up regularly and plan to keep suitable fire extinguishing equipment on board – and easily accessible. This is part of the RCD and the BSS regulations: it does not just apply to finished craft.

Contact details
RCD: A good starting base is the Royal Yachting Association (RYA) – this is a very readable outline, much better than the 'official' version: click on the *general guidance* link.
www.rya.org.uk/KnowledgeBase/ technical/reccraftdir.htm
BSS: Effectively administered by British Waterways and the Environment Agency; this is a useful source of information and ideas to ensure safety of the craft and its crew. There are a lot of technical references, which a boat fitter really needs to understand. If in any doubt, always seek advice.
www.boatsafetyscheme.com

David Bulmer opted to finish the fitting-out of his narrowboat tug, *Lyra*. The shell was built by Jonathan Wilson and initial fitting done by Dursley and Hurst.

Thinking outside the usual: stove, circular shower, ship windows

"This was not a sailaway in the conventional sense, it was supplied two thirds complete from the builder. However, nearly all of the finishes are mine, as well as the detailing plus the back cabin.

Standard sailaways are plentiful but not everyone is willing to be flexible enough to build it your way, particularly if the shell supplier is not their preferred one.

You need to find a good builder who will work with your ideas – in my case we worked on a budget but came in under it so I was pleasantly surprised."

His Top Tips

1 It may look easy but there is an enormous amount of work involved – you only need to look at the wiring or plumbing on any boat to gain an appreciation of the complexity.
2 Don't underestimate the time element, you need to allocate many weeks or even years to complete the job and that takes perseverance and commitment.
3 The idea of a self build might be appealing to save money and that is no doubt possible, however, much of the cost of any boat whether professionally built or self built is materials. They all need the hull, engine, toilet, fridge cooker etc, and the pro has the advantage of trade pricing. Not to say discounts are not available to anyone, but on balance the pricing favours the pro.
4 Think outside of the conventions when it comes to materials. For instance my side windows are from a ship breaker's yard in Bangladesh. They are superb quality and very heavy. They cost little more than conventional windows and I bought bronze portholes to match. These were new but designed for sea use so the glass is much thicker, so less condensation. But then I had the problem of finding matching brass dome headed bolts to fit them and they took some tracking down.
5 Similar thing with my circular glass shower, I have not seen one quite like this on any boat. We had to mount it right down on the hull cross members to accommodate the height. Most things can be done but they need thinking through.

There are a number of examples of what I am saying: for instance my antique enamelled stove I found on ebay – being round, the heat comes out all ways and the sides of the boat don't get hot so you don't need to tile the sides. As long as these less conventional ideas still meet the Boat Safety Scheme rules you are fine.

Get some basics installed early on so that you can make a cuppa – you'll need it!

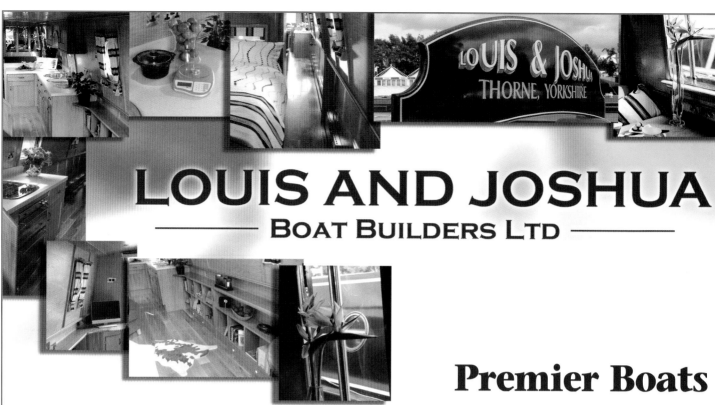

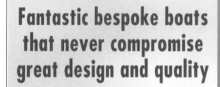

Buying a used boat

With so many boats to choose from, finding the right one can be tricky. We offer some expert advice to help you

Tidy galley area on a little 30ft boat

This 1980s interior looks slightly dated these days

This 50ft semi-trad is a good example of a practical and well kept ex-hire boat

Buying a secondhand boat is like buying a secondhand car – except ten times more expensive. Unfortunately, just as in car buying, it is easy to let one's heart rule one's head but the consequences can equally be ten times more expensive. Which means that you need to be ten times more careful.

WHAT TO BUY

First piece of advice about used boat buying is the same we would give to new boat buyers. Gather information: get plans and sales details, visit boats at brokerages and shows to see how different layouts work in practice. Think about getting right through the boat in an emergency, how using the toilet/shower/galley will affect people moving through the boat and where your guests will sit in the open. Most important of all, involve your partner otherwise you might get a quick course in single-handing!

Think about the use you will put the boat to and the equipment you may need – for example, a liveaboard will need complex electrical systems and extra batteries which will up the price. You may not need them on a 'weekend' boat.

Talk to other boatowners, read internet

newsgroups and other boat related sites and do not be afraid to ask for advice – you will probably get too much, a lot conflicting. Download or send for the latest Boat Safety Scheme regulations, study and learn them. This will allow you to judge the validity of a boat's certificate.

Then finally, before you start looking at boats with an intention to actually purchase, visit any local housebuilders who are renovating old properties. Ask them if they have any wet or dry rot that you can smell. You need to remember this musty, mushroomy smell!

WHERE TO BUY

There are, essentially, two sources of used boats: private sellers and brokerages. Just as in buying a used car privately, it's very much a case of 'caveat emptor' or 'buyer beware' – the onus is on you to check the condition of the boat and verify the owner's claims for it.

A broker acts as a sort of estate agent and will offer boats for sale on behalf of their owners. They will produce written and, usually, internet details, handle offers and arrange things like finance and surveys for the buyer. A good broker will ask for

detailed information from the owner but cannot guarantee the owner's honesty in supplying this, so again, facts need to be checked. And remember, however helpful they are, they're working for the seller, not the buyer!

Be aware from the outset in boat buying that there is no formal proof of ownership like a car's logbook so legal ownership will need to be checked out. Expect to see a bill of sale from the previous owner and other back-up evidence such as mooring and maintenance bills etc. Likewise you need to check for outstanding finance (which can be done through a credit checking service like HPI) especially when buying privately. You'll need a valid Boat Safety Certificate and a newer craft will need to conform to the Recreational Craft Directive (RCD) as well – see Chapter 4 'Buying a new boat'.

It is also absolutely essential to have a full professional survey done on a boat you are thinking of buying but at this stage you are committing sizeable sums of money: if you are dealing with a broker you will be asked for a deposit of around ten per cent which may only be returnable if significant faults are found. In addition a survey will cost around £600-£750, including the cost of having the boat dry-docked.

Therefore you need to do your own detective work first so you are at least reasonably sure of what you are about to spend money on. Here's how to go about it.

THE OUTSIDE

First impressions count – but make sure you look beyond the superficial gloss or grime at the shell below. Today's 'name' builders are well known but companies come and go in this industry over the years so you will need to research older builders and develop an eye for comparing boats.

Shells come in a variety of "qualities". Bottom of the range will always fetch low prices however good you make them look; a top range hull bought in poor condition will fetch a good price once you smarten it. Use the sales sheet to get an impression of hull quality. Chapter 12 goes into shell construction in detail but, generally, when it comes to metal thickness, the bigger the numbers the better. Typically better quality hulls also have longer swims (the "pointy" bits at either end). Expect them to be between six and eight feet long on a mid-range hull.

Inspect the welds on the cabin sides. Cheap boats will have wavy cabin sides and the welds standing proud. Mid-range hulls will have the welds ground flush, but you will still see indentations unless someone has filled them with body. Top-class hulls should have no visible welds and the cabin sides should be absolutely flat. You may also find nice details that show off the builder's skills. You should now be able to tell if the price of the boat reflects its underlying value.

Inspect the hull for signs of rust pitting. Look around the waterline and below any vents in the hull (sink/basin drain, gas tank drain, and exhaust). On a modern hull pits of less than 0.5mm or so should cause no concern. A few larger ones can be filled with weld when the boat is being blacked. Check the anodes (silvery lumps of metal welded to the hull just underwater by a steel bar, often two at the front and back). Very pitted and eroded anodes or missing anodes indicate poor maintenance and cost cutting in the past.

Check the hull specification to confirm the seller's claims for it. Borrow (or buy – £12 from Screwfix) a 0 to 25mm micrometer. You are only interested in measuring to the nearest mm which is easy. Measure the thickness through the drains for the front cockpit and through engine room vents or where the gunwales turns over in the cockpit. Measure the roof and cabin side where it overhangs at the front or back. In all these cases allow say 0.5 mm for paint thickness. If the boat is ashore you can measure the base plate "overhang" where it joins the hull sides – expect some wear.

Now inspect the cabin sides and roof. Areas of rust that are not very pitted may lower the price but as long as they are in full view, they are repairable during painting. If, however, you see rust bubbles emanating from (say) behind a window frame there is a problem. Unless you take the frame out, fully treat the rust and repaint, the rust will keep creeping out from below the frame, and as the steel below the frame rusts it expands, pushing the frame away from the side, giving rise to leaks.

Look inside cockpit lockers and all round the engine room to ensure the inside of the hull is not badly pitted.

THE INTERIOR

Walk through the boat sniffing and looking around windows, chimneys and roof vents. Wet cloth and rot smells tells you there is a problem with the woodwork. "Toilet" smells may indicate a lack of cleanliness or it may indicate a leaking toilet tank, low-quality toilet hoses or even a gas leak.

Black streaks in the wood or "water marks", bowing gaps, delamination of plywood or blockboard and swelling MDF all indicate present or past water leaks. At the same time look for signs of "Conti-board" or other chipboard. This is not suitable for damp environments. Good-quality fit-outs will use solid wood and possibly plywood, whilst cheaper fit outs use a lot of MDF – look in the base of any routered features. If it's a uniform brown with no marked grain it's MDF.

Look in the internal channels of the windows. If they are full of moss etc the long term care of the boat is suspect, as it is if rubber cord is pulled out of place (between glass and frame) and is lying across the corners of the window.

Check the electric wiring carefully. Unscrew a switch or speaker so you can check the type and thickness of thermal insulation. Look under the gunwales and in the back of cupboards to find the wiring. This should be clipped up in neat bundles and if any individual cable feels stiff when bent between two fingers and the thumb it is probably solid strand domestic cable that will fracture in time. If you find any flat three-strand mains cable (not mains flex) it is again an indication of poor fitting out unless it is a very old boat.

Light every gas burner and ensure they all work and none burns with a yellow flame. If the fridge is gas then light that and again ensure there is no yellow in the flame. Test all electrical equipment. The more that does not work, the worse the boat has been looked after. Turn on a number of lights and operate the water pump or electric toilet, if the lights dim noticeably there is a problem. If it's not flat batteries it is probably expensive and may be dangerous.

Now turn your attention to the bilges. Most boats built over the last 20 years will be of the two-bilge design with an accommodation bilge that is separated from the engine or stern bilge but there are a few exceptions. Older boats may have "all in one" bilges, a front, accommodation, and engine bilge (again separate) or the front bilge may be piped through the accommodation bilge into the engine bilge.

At the back of the cabin, usually under the steps or in a cupboard, there should be a trap to give access to the accommodation bilge. The bilge should be dry in an insulated boat. If it is not it indicates leaking, possibly windows, water system, toilet system, or shower/bath system and pump. If it's the latter you may well see soap scum or smell the soap. If you have turned the water pump on and you hear it running now and again it may well indicate a domestic water leak. If the water is clear and the pump is silent then it is probably condensation or window leaks. Very often this is the area where wood rot can be found

You can expect the baseplate to be rusty on an older boat and it is of little consequence unless either the baseplate is thin or deeply pitted (say

Mould in window runners: a sign of poor maintenance

Blackening of timber is evidence of damp penetration

Single core domestic cables should not be seen in boats

Rust creeping out from under windows is hard to cure

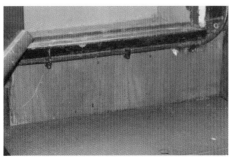
This board covered rot caused by leaking door

More lack of care – a window rubber has pulled out

Unusual boats like this one from Jannel are difficult to price and can be hard to sell

Typical galley on a mid-range 1990s boat

1mm +). There should not be any wet carpet or floor covering in this area. If there is water present or wet floor coverings then question the maintenance.

THE ENGINE

Now look at the engine – make it clear to the vendor/broker that you will be running the engine and checking the gearbox.

Look into the engine coolant header tank. The level should be at least an inch below the filler neck, but it can be far lower as long as you can see the coolant. It should not be thick and brown like cocoa, the colour of the anti-freeze should be visible. Very rusty, "thick" water indicates a lack of maintenance and possible corrosion inside the cooling system.

Run your hand over the batteries and engine. If you feel warmth make another appointment and insist that the batteries are not charged or the engine started without you being present. If there are any explanations or excuses as to why the batteries needed charging just before viewing or why they are flat, question the charging system and estimate between £60 and £120 per battery for new ones.

The engine should start easily from cold and any white smoke should stop after a few minutes. If the engine is equipped with heater/glow plugs allow up to 30 seconds for these to do their job. The longer it takes to start and the more/longer it smokes the worse condition the engine is in.

Move the control lever to ahead and rev the engine. Note how long it takes for the propeller shaft to start to rotate. Repeat with reverse. Both should take similar time for the shaft to come up to speed and the longer it takes the more chance the gearbox is worn out. A clang or thud as the gears engage may indicate a faulty drive plate or gearbox. Leave the engine running.

Inspect the batteries. If they have grown "fur" on the terminals the boat has not been well looked after. If the end of any battery is bowing out and swelling the battery is nearing the end of its life. The larger the bow, the shorter its remaining life.

At either side of the engine and behind it there is a bilge where there may be a little water but there should be no oil. If the whole area is covered in black oil with pieces of dirt or rag floating in it the boat has not been well looked after. Under the engine there should be a sealed area. I would like to see this clean and free from all oil and water. A bilge blanket here to absorb and oil or fuel drips shows care.

Again if this area is full of oil and water the boat has not been maintained very well. Ideally the whole of the area should be well painted with little signs of rust, a film of dust and the odd oily area is acceptable.

Ex-hire boats are usually very well maintained and can prove to be good buys for the family boater, offering plenty of accommodation

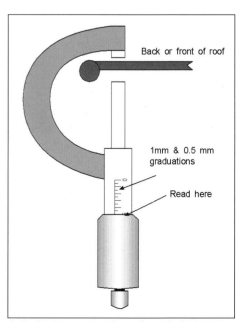
A simple micrometer can be used to make basic checks on the thickness of narrowboat steek panels

Small boats like this 33ft cruiser can provide a reasonably inexpensive introduction to canal boating

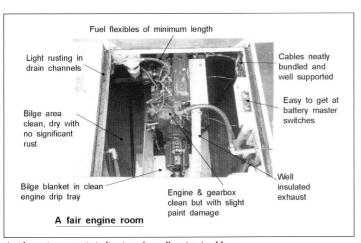

Fuel flexibles of minimum length

Light rusting in drain channels

Cables neatly bundled and well supported

Easy to get at battery master switches

Bilge area clean, dry with no significant rust

Bilge blanket in clean engine drip tray

Engine & gearbox clean but with slight paint damage

Well insulated exhaust

A fair engine room

A tidy engine room is indicative of a well maintained boat. Here is our checklist of what to watch out for

The evergreen Springer is enduringly popular despite its advancing years – this one is a 23ft example

WHAT YOU GET FOR YOUR MONEY

Cost (£)	Boat
100	Basic canoe or 8ft rowing boat
600	New three person inflatable and 3hp outboard motor
1,000	16ft, second-hand GRP cruiser, with 7.5hp outboard and small two berth cabin
3,500	30-year-old, 25ft, GRP canal cruiser, with 10hp outboard – basic but useable
7,500	20+-year-old, 23ft, all steel outboard powered mini-narrowboat
9,000	27ft, River cruiser with diesel inboard, from early 1970s
15,000	Basic 30ft narrowboat, around 20-25 years old
20,000	20-30-year-old, 30-40ft, steel narrowboat, variable condition, usually cruiser
30,000	Tidy ten-year-old, 40ft trad, older 40-50ft cruiser
40,000	Most well-equipped early 1990s, 50ft narrowboat
50,000	Early 1990s, 55-60ft, well-equipped trad, mid-80s 70 footer
60,000	60ft, well-equipped boat from major builder, under ten years old
75,000	Exceptional one-owner narrowboat, 60-70ft, widebeam
75,000+	Widebeams, high luxury or top-end replica narrowboats

These prices are a guide only: actual prices depend on condition, shell quality, fit-out and equipment. Older cruiser stern boats are generally cheaper than trad or semi-trad of similar age.

There should be no major oil or rust streaks on the engine, no build up of oily dirt and no pools of oil or water on it.

Now the engine is getting warm, take the oil filler cap off and rev the engine. There will be a certain amount of pressure coming from the filler (compare with other boats and even your car) but excess pressure or smoky fumes indicate engine problems. If there is a pressure gauge check the oil pressure. On a modern engine (not air cooled Listers) expect more than 15psi on idle and over 35psi when revving when hot.

Stop the engine, pause, and check the engine and gearbox dipstick for level. The engine oil should be fairly black but runny. Water gives oils a whitish tinge, this is a bad sign. Smell the engine oil, if you can smell diesel there is a problem.

Finally, take the boat for a run. If a river is nearby give it a bit of an upstream thrash to ensure the engine does not overheat or make excessive smoke. Compare the vibration, noise and stopping ability with the boats you hired.

If you are still satisfied, it is time to make an offer subject to survey and make sure it is understood that final price is dependant upon the survey.

Now you only have to find a legal mooring!

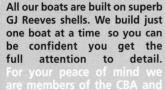

How to plan your new boat

If you want to buy a made-to-measure new boat then spend time planning and researching the subject as there are many different possibilities in layout and style

This versatile rear space can provide either two single berths or daytime seating space near the steerer

This long, 65ft boat offers versatile accommodation for up to six but at the expense of go-anywhere cruising ability

Like that old joke about the yokel giving instructions to someone who is lost "well, if I was going there, I wouldn't start from here!" when it comes to designing a boat for long distance cruising, not many people would start with a metal tube that's 70 feet long by seven feet wide.

Today's cruising narrowboat is an accident of history. Never in James Brindley's or Thomas Telford's wildest imaginings could they have thought that their 18th century transport medium would become a 21st century leisure pursuit. The narrow gauge canals, locks, bridges and tunnels they built were purely a commercial expedient but they are now the fundamental design constraints when it comes to planning a narrowboat. (Wider beam boats we will talk about later.)

So let's just reiterate what they are. The maximum length and width of locks are the key: on the majority of the system these will take a boat that is approximately 70ft long by 7ft wide – in fact old working boats slightly longer than 70ft can just squeeze in.

However, today's boats are pretty universally built to slightly under seven feet – 6ft 10ins is the norm to allow for movement in lock structures over the years that have caused walls to bulge inwards and so on.

Length is more a matter of choice: 70 feet is the absolute maximum and therefore offers the greatest cabin space but it will restrict cruising routes as not all locks will take the longest boats. Several of the northern canals have wider, shorter locks. Hence the 'go anywhere' dimension is 57ft 6in by 6ft 10in. A boat that is longer than this will still have a large number of cruising options but will miss out on such spectacular routes as the Leeds & Liverpool canal.

It should be remembered, too, that the longer the boat, the trickier it is to manoeuvre, moor and turn – and the more expensive it will be to licence and find a marina mooring for, as these are governed by length. A longer boat is necessarily also going to have a smaller market when it comes to sell as well.

Length, then, is the key consideration. The obvious decision is to plumb for that go-anywhere 57ft 6in maximum and, indeed, the majority of new boats are now being built at or close to that length. Size has gradually crept up over the years as people have expected more from their new build (and been prepared to spend more money on it.)

But before following the crowd, it is worth giving some thought to whether you actually need a full-size boat. Remember, steel (and therefore boat) prices have risen sharply, licence fees are likely to keep rising as government aid to the waterways is reduced and moorings are in short supply – and expensive.

A smaller boat of, say, 40 to 50ft can save money, find moorings where others cannot and be easier to handle. It can also provide more than adequate accommodation – especially if being principally used for 'weekending' rather than extended cruising or living aboard.

On the other hand – and there's always an 'other hand' in narrowboat design – a longer boat is generally more space efficient. There are certain fixed lengths in a shell whatever its overall size: rear deck, engine bay, minimum front deck, so a longer boat will have proportionately more cabin space compared to overall length than a short one.

The remaining shell dimensions of height, cabin width, headroom and draft have become something of a 'given' in the industry, though if you have firm, sensible ideas, you should be able to discuss things with your shell builder (for example, we know of one customer who specified a vee rather than flat bottom and slightly reduced cabin height for a boat that was to be moored on the Mon & Brec Canal where bridges are tight and the canal itself is shallow.)

The planning process is worth spending plenty

This luxuriously fitted out widebeam Henley Apartment Boat has as much room as many a London flat

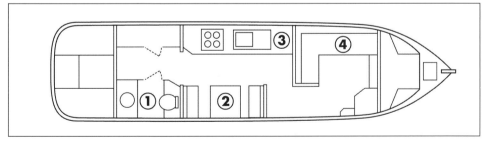

This 31ft Sea Otter maximises its internal space through versatile fittings
1 Wetroom shower 2 Dinette converts to single bed 3 Galley 4 Saloon sofa converts to double berth

The traditional boatman's cabin delights enthusiasts and can be incorporated in a new design

of time on – and take plenty of advice from builders and other owners as well. It's a bit like juggling: you have to keep several balls in the air at the same time. Elements of the boat can't be looked at in isolation: you need to try and consider the whole 'package'. You may decide you want a long tug front deck, semi-trad rear deck, dinette, full length bed, cabin for the kids, large galley and a nice bath. Well add that lot up and you'll find yourself in a 75ft long boat not a 57ft long one!

Before you start deciding on the layout of the galley and colour of the armchairs, absolutely the first consideration is to decide what you want your boat for. This may seem obvious but a confusion of priorities here can cause deep dissatisfaction later. For example, many people think they should have a boat they can take friends, children, grandchildren on for breaks or holidays. So they plan in secondary accommodation at the expense of living or galley space – and then find it is rarely used. Perhaps a pump-up inflatable bed would have been quite adequate.

Alternatively, people are scared by the cost of inverters, extra batteries and big alternators – then find they can't run a much-needed washing machine during extended cruising.

Ask yourself some proper questions – and ask them of other boaters, too. Do you want an engine room and boatman's cabin at the expense of 14ft of space in the boat? Do you like traditional portholes

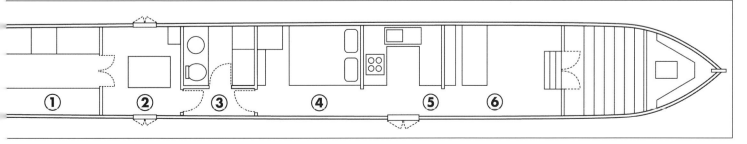

The boatman's cabin and engine room configuration is a traditional but practical layout
1 Boatman's cabin with folding bed and stove 2 Engine room 3 Bathroom 4 Main cabin 5 Galley 6 Saloon

Traditionally the most popular layout is this arrangement with the cabin at the rear of the boat – this one with a cross double – though it may not be a layout that is best suited to busy boats

Some boatfitters have experimented in materials other than wood but the results don't always seem successful

enough to not mind the reduced light in the cabin?

Is the little trad deck sufficient when mates will be on board most weekends? And what about the dogs – where will they go?

The best piece of advice comes (as it usually does) from a boatbuilder who said 'plan your boat for yourself, not for other people'. In other words, don't short-change what you want from it to deal with the 'ifs', 'buts' and 'maybes'.

INTERIOR LAYOUTS

We look at the design of the shell itself in detail in Chapter 12 and choices made there in rear deck design, length of the forward deck and window style will impact upon the space of the interior but, ultimately, there remains a fixed amount of space inside the boat that has to be shared out amongst various 'units' – some of them pretty rigid in their requirements and others more flexible.

What we are attempting to accommodate in a modern boat are a saloon (or lounge), a cabin (bedroom), galley (kitchen) and bathroom. Beyond this we might be looking for additional sleeping space, dedicated eating space, a utility area, office space, an engine room in a traditional boat and a boatman's cabin or some modern evolution of this.

Because of its width, the narrowboat has to have a one-room-after-another layout but even so, there are a great many variations on the theme. The most common one is, from the front, the saloon, followed by a galley, then bathroom, cabin and engine bay (either under the steps up to a trad deck or under the deck itself on a cruiser or semi-trad.) It's a configuration that fits easily into everything from 45ft upwards, with the saloon and galley being the areas most readily stretched or shrunk. On shorter boats, spaces have to be shared – usually by the sofa converting to a bed at night.

Once above 50ft, fitting a fixed 'dinette' between the saloon and galley becomes a practicality. This cuts into saloon space but provides convivial 'family' eating space, rather than perching on armchairs or pulling out foldaway table and chairs. It also converts easily into a second double bed, a sensible distance from the main cabin. (Secondary

sleeping space is possible without a dinette, using a convertible fixed sofa, as we shall see later, or chair-beds in the saloon.

As length increases towards 60ft so more possibilities are opened up and the design becomes more flexible: a small office space can be built in, often adjacent to the cabin for quietness, or a utility space added for a washing machine and second toilet.

All in all this is a popular and well-proven configuration. The saloon offers easy access to the front deck for socialising – and a cratch cover with glass front and perspex side panels can be built over this deck to create a sort of conservatory effect. A small fold down or stowaway table is often added to enable alfresco dining here too.

The galley becomes the heart of the boat, as it is the heart of most homes, with the bathroom and toilet easily accessed from front and rear.

The downside to this layout is that the steerer can become isolated from all those people having an enjoyable beer on the front deck and access to and from the rear deck is straight through the main cabin. Imagine that in wet weather or after being out on a muddy towpath.

As a result, an alternative on boats with a lot of pedestrian 'traffic' through them puts the galley at the rear immediately ahead of the rear deck. This only works with a semi-trad or cruiser design where the engine is under the rear deck: in a trad the engine and the steps down into the boat sit where the galley would be (a remote engine with hydraulic drive would still enable this option – at a cost) though people traffic to and from the rear shouldn't be such an issue in a trad.

The typical rear galley layout, then, would place the galley typically either side ahead of the rear steps, (perhaps preceded by a utility or wet-locker room) and followed by the dinette if fitted, saloon, bathroom and finally a front cabin. With the social space majoring at the rear of the boat the front deck would probably not need to be large or covered.

An alternative layout, though less popular, would be to have the saloon at the rear, galley centrally and cabin at the front – something which is achievable, though not necessarily desirable in all stern designs.

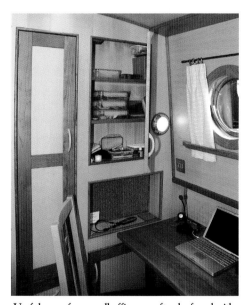

Useful space for a small office can often be found with some careful planning – this is in a corner of the cabin

Ultra-compact second toilet fitted in Aqualine boat

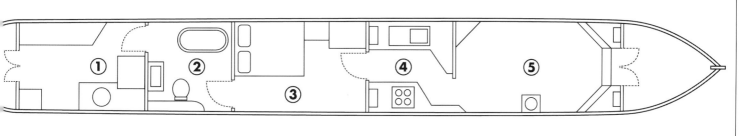

This rather unusual central cabin layout was designed for a liveaboard and features a particularly large bathroom
1 Utility area 2 Bathroom 3 Cabin 4 Galley 5 Saloon

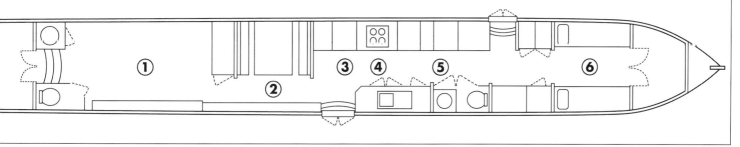

This 65ft boat was designed for maximum possible versatility with two toilets and two shower rooms. Both saloons can be converted to bedrooms
1 Saloon (small toilet room in corner) 2 Convertible dinette 3 Second shower 4 Galley 5 Bathroom 6 Front cabin/day lounge

This large cruiser stern has a sensible grille to keep children, or dogs, safe

The minimalist, loft-style look now popular for many narrowboat interiors, using white ash for the lining-out

THE BOATMAN'S CABIN

The boatman's cabin is the traditionalist's delight, recalling as it does the days of the working canal boats when the boatman (and his family!) would live in this tiny but remarkably well organised space.

The true boatman's cabin, accessed from the rear deck, is approximately eight feet long. It incorporates a stove, a drop-out curved end table that forms the door of a cupboard unit and a small bench seat. Opposite this is the 'bed 'ole' whose door drops down and links with the bench to form a three-quarter width cross bed, the mattress being stowed inside the 'ole when not in use. Everything is finished in traditional colours, patterns and most notably a scumbling – or graining – paint effect.

The cabin is generally allied to an engine room sitting immediately ahead and proudly displaying a highly-polished vintage engine, though boatman's cabins, or variations on them, can be seen – generally in smaller boats – without the engine room as the two features do take up something over 14 feet of interior space. (It's not wasted space, of course, the bed can be 'tweaked' to more or less double width and used either as main or secondary accommodation, and the engine room is a good place to dry wet gear and store miscellaneous junk.)

Even non-traditionalists can see the merits of a boatman's cabin: it provides a cosy space at the rear of the boat, means that the steerer is not always isolated, can offer extra sleeping space and can stop wet and dirty boaters passing through the cabin.

As a result, there have been some clever modern variations on the theme, usually based around bench seats that can be jiggled into various bed arrangements when needed.

THE WALK THROUGH

Some boats seem immediately more interesting than others when you step aboard and it's not just because of lavish timberwork. The narrowboat, as we know, is long and thin and the designs which work best are those that break this space up: correspondingly, the least satisfactory are those that take the eye virtually straight from front to back of the boat.

There aren't too many options. Almost

The mid-size aluminium Sea Otter boats are carefully planned internally to offer maximum space

Storage space is always at a premium on a boat so plan wardrobes and cupboards carefully

The traditional tongue and groove pine is less popular for lining-out these days, but it does remain handsome, especially when diagonally as here, and is very 'boaty'

universally, you enter a boat centrally at the front and exit centrally at the rear. The simplest route between the two is a corridor down the middle, but it's one that looks bleak and isn't very efficient. The beds have to be singles, and the bathroom and toilet split into tiny units (or closing across the corridor blocking access along it). Only tall people will appreciate it!

The obvious alternative, enabling a double bed and decent size bathroom is a side corridor, but here headroom and shoulder room can be tight, which leads us to the third option, a mixture of one and two: a central walkway through the lounge (logical since it's the most open plan) a side gangway past the cabin and perhaps the bathroom and a linking section between the two, around which the galley is formed in various ways. As the galley and dinette, if included, contain the most cabinetry, this allows the good designer to break the lines of the interior up and show off his joinery skills.

THE FIT-OUT

The vast majority of narrowboats are fitted out in wood – it's a 'boaty' material, suits the bespoke nature of the industry and affords numerous options in fashion and finish. Other materials have been tried: wipe clean laminates, glass-fibre, man-made fabrics and more, but in the end it generally all comes back to wood.

But which wood? Boat interiors have been very influenced by domestic interior fashions. Pine tongue and grooving was pretty commonplace in the 1970s and '80s for cladding walls and 'boxing-in' so it was widely used for lining out boats, particularly as it was so easy to install.

It is still favoured by some DIY boatfitters but disadvantages are that, unless cleverly done, it only emphasises the long, thin nature of the boat and it also darkens greatly with age, which can make interiors gloomy.

These days, lining out is typically done in veneered ply sheets, using solid wood 'trims' to cover the joins and provide the decoration. It's a relatively fast and efficient method.

Choice of wood finish is down to the buyer and, right now, light coloured woods like ash are popular, echoing the minimalist 'loft style' apartments of the colour supplements. Perhaps one day they will appear as dated as t&g does today? Oak remains a popular, more conservative choice,

while beech and cherry are also good looking, regularly used woods.

Cabinetry carcassing tends to be in blockboard or thicker ply, with cut edges trimmed with the appropriate hardwood and solid doors, but on very expensive fit-outs solid wood may be used almost throughout.

The one product that gets a bad press is MDF, which will deteriorate if exposed to water. For that reason, many boatfitters refuse to use it. Others say it is perfectly acceptable if used correctly – citing the fact that it is widely used in building domestic kitchen units. It's certainly easy to use; it can be cut or routered into curves and other intricate shapes, and doesn't distort as 'real' wood can.

The truth is probably somewhere in between the two arguments: MDF should not be used in areas exposed to damp but ought to be okay in kitchen or saloon cabinets – unless the boat is likely to be left unattended, unheated and therefore prone to dampness for periods of time.

A WORD ABOUT WIDEBEAMS

There are typically two 'widebeam'-style boats – the 'wide narrowboat' and the Dutch barge. The wide narrowboat is typically around 10 to 11ft wide and tends to be laid out similarly to the narrowboat: it simply has more width, allowing greater space for the individual compartments.

The Dutch barge comes in a greater variety of configurations. Popular is the centre wheelhouse type, which provides for a double cabin, perhaps en suite, to the rear of the wheelhouse and the main galley, saloon and, if desired, a second cabin forward of the wheelhouse. Sometimes these are accessed by separate stairways; other versions have a walkway through from front to rear under the wheelhouse floor.

The alternative barge has its wheelhouse to the rear with all the sleeping and day areas forwards of this. Both versions come in a variety of widths and lengths, enabling a great deal of variation in layout.

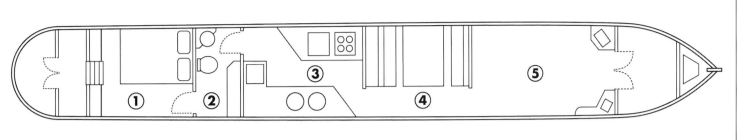

The rear cabin is almost the standard narrowboat layout – this example also featuring a through bathroom
1 Cabin 2 Bathroom 3 Galley 4 Convertible dinette 5 Saloon

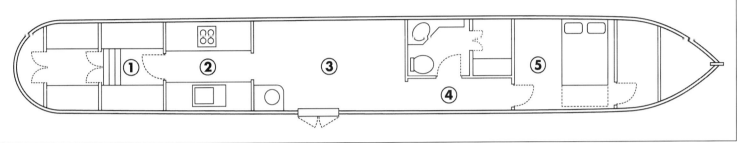

The most popular alternative is the rear galley layout which keeps the cabin private
1 Utility/office 2 Galley 3 Saloon 4 Bathroom 5 Cabin

THE PLANNING PROCESS

Once you have read through the next few chapters on the individual sections of the boat you should be in a position to start planning your own. This can be done the old-fashioned way, with a big pad of square paper and a pencil or, if you have access to it, a basic computer-aided design programme.

But before you start, remember that if the wonderful design idea you have thought of has not been done before it's probably not the Holy Grail in narrowboat planning, more likely the fool's gold!

As always in planning, you need to start with your most rigid elements and work towards your most flexible – you can't adjust the amount of space a cooker needs but you can adjust the length of the saloon.

You will need room around items as well – space to use the cooker, dry yourself in the bathroom and so on. Any good kitchen planning guide will help you with dimensions of components and the space needed around them, while a handy book, *The Architect's Pocketbook* provides guideline measurements for everything from armchairs to baths.

When sketching out your thoughts it is important to remember where the systems will run in your boat. Generally boatbuilders will aim to keep everything close together and accessible for service or repair, and also minimise pipe and heavy-load cable lengths. A bathroom at one end of the boat and galley at the other poses obvious plumbing complications, as would having the sink on the starboard side and basin or shower on the port.

If you are fitting your own boat out you will need to do extensive drawings to firm up pipe and cable runs, ascertain locations of windows and hatches, position large items such as the calorifier, ensure that the boat is well balanced by proper positioning of tanks and so on. If you simply want to be in a position to discuss things with a boatbuilder, then simpler plans will be sufficient – a builder will be able to offer worthwhile suggestions and improvements. That's what you are paying him for after all.

A less common arrangement sees the main saloon at the rear of the boat with the main cabin up front

The rear galley layout is very practical. It keeps wet or dirty outdoor wear away from the living areas of the boat

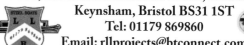

The saloon

This is the room in which the long-term boater will spend most of their time so we look at ways to make it as comfortable and cosy as your living room at home

The ultimate in narrowboating luxury? A stunning art-deco interior from Fernwood

Anyone browsing through some recent issues of *Canal Boat* magazine could be forgiven for thinking that the saloon takes no sort of designing skill at all: it's simply an empty room with a couple of easy chairs in it, a stove in one corner and a TV in the other.

To a certain extent that is true. Free-standing furniture has certainly become a very popular option with boat buyers; taking over in large part from the fitted saloon furniture that was formerly so common.

It's easy to see why: there are some very stylish and comfortable reclining chairs on the market right now from companies such as Stressless, and if you're in a boat intended for two then a pair of these makes perfect sense. They can be moved around if needs be and augmented with fold-away chairs if you have guests. Do be careful, though, that you don't buy seats so large that they dwarf a small lounge.

Likewise take care if putting a domestic sofa into a boat – many are simply too bulky and if placed lengthways appear to half-fill the saloon space. If you want a sofa, have a small two-seater and a good idea is to place it across the width of the boat. This immediately creates a feeling of extra space in the room. It means that your field of vision, instead of being only as far as the opposite cabin wall about four feet away, is down the length of the boat for ten feet or more.

One of the main reasons for choosing fixed furniture was that it could be readily adapted for sleeping purposes but the advent of cleverly-designed chair beds and bed-settees especially created for boats has got around that issue too.

Fixed furniture has lost out because the more basic types found in older hire boats simply weren't comfortable enough. They were pushed hard up against the hull side so that you were forced to sit rigidly upright with your head almost pushed forwards by the cabin side.

The other problem is that if the sofa is to convert to a bed it will need a flat cushion base to form the mattress whereas a comfortable sofa cushion needs an element of angle to it or a 'roll' at its front. It is possible to get around this with well-designed

This sofa looks uncomfortably upright and illustrates a problem that can be found with fixed furniture

This small cross-sofa fits comfortably in the narrowboat and makes the saloon feel much larger, too

Clever flaps turn this pullman dinette into a six seater and store away under gunwale

Modern flat screen TVs take up little space. This one swings out for easy viewing

cushions but care must be taken. And even the good fixed sofas rarely seem to be as comfortable for lazy lounging as reclining chair and a footstool.

So are there *any* advantages then in fixed furniture? The chief one is that they can allow the boat to have a proper table without the need for an additional dinette. A table top with either fold-out legs or separate 'Desmo'-type legs can be stowed away under a gunwale and brought out when needed and used with the sofa.

Since four or even six people can be comfortably seated around the TV or the table, fixed sofas work well on family or social boats. Sitting round a table to enjoy a meal with friends or family is something that can be enjoyed as much on a boat as at home. Somehow it doesn't seem the same perched on fold-up chairs or eating, TV-dinner fashion, in your armchairs.

They are, as we said, easily adapted into double berths – a popular method on L-shaped sofas is by pulling out infill slats with the backrest cushion forming the second part of the mattress – and they also provide very useful underseat storage.

Finally, fixed furniture doesn't fall about: you probably will not be intending to put to sea in your boat, but a trip on a rough tidal river section could see your loose furniture sliding around.

If there is room in the boat then a fixed dinette area can be combined with free-standing saloon seating. The pullman dinette – bench seats either side of a table – is the commonest choice. In a busy boat a neat device is to have small extensions to the seats and table so that six rather than four people can sit comfortably at the table: these are either folded away or clipped under the gunwale when not in use.

The dinette unit is almost invariably raised on a plinth so that people sitting at the table can easily see out of a side window. At night the table top is dropped down into position between the seats to form the base of a double bed.

The seat 'boxes' provide considerable storage space under the seat cushions, although a good deal of this will probably be taken up with holding the bedding for the dinette conversion. Sometimes one seat box can be used to hold, for example, a small pull-out freezer box. The plinth itself offers a certain amount of additional stowage as well. In many boat interiors the dinette is used as a major design element with a full-height and nicely sculptured divider separating the living area from the galley and beyond.

Most boaters now want to cruise with all their home comforts and that usually includes a television and a decent hi-fi. Fortunately miniaturisation of components has made building these into the saloon a great deal easier. Flat-screen TVs in particular, have become very popular and, if you haven't got as far down the road as iPods for music storage, then cds and dvds are still small and easily stowed.

By the way, don't invest several hundred pounds in the latest flat screen TV without a proper aerial to match – these range from costly self-adjusting satellite finders to more simple affairs that have to be moved into positon by hand.

The under-gunwales space, sometimes wasted on boats, is ideal for the sort of shallow cupboards or shelves that can accommodate books, cds and the like, and a flat screen TV can also be installed here – generally hidden from prying eyes behind a movable panel.

A typical and attractive design links this under gunwale unit to a corner cupboard at the front of the saloon. A radiator is often built into this area as well and hopefully (but not always) nicely boxed in.

In many saloon layouts the corner cupboard is complemented by a stove on the other side of the doorway. This is a convenient location, keeping the hot stove out of trafficked areas in the boat but the downside is that the heat is being produced right at one end of the boat when it would be more logical to have it nearer the centreline. A central location does impose significant design constraints, though, since furniture and fittings must be kept clear of its hot surfaces.

THE CRATCH

The front deck can be used as a pleasant extension of the saloon if it is fitted with a cratch and cover. The cratch frame normally has glass panels for a good forward view and the roll-up side panels can also have transparent sections in them.

The cratch does make getting at the forward gas locker tricky so the frame is often hinged to ease access. A cratch may also reduce boat security since it can allow a thief the opportunity to work unseen when attempting to break open the front door.

The last, but certainly not the least thing to consider when planning the saloon, is the floor covering. A fitted carpet, often extending up the hull sides as far as the gunwales, is commonly used over a ply base floor but wooden 'plank' floors have become increasingly popular, just as they have in domestic use.

They certainly look attractive and are easier to keep clean in a boat than a carpet but the downside is that they are much colder underfoot.

A covered foredeck makes a pleasant place to sit out. The fold down table is a handy extra

This versatile sofa is used with under-gunwale table top for dining and converts to bed

Individual reclining armchairs like these from Stressless have become very popular

The galley

If you are looking to live on board or go long-term cruising, a well equipped galley is a top priority. We run through the design and equipment possibilities

A purpose-designed full height pull-out larder cupboard is a very space-efficient method of storage

Finding a spot to store the wine is always a priority on board and a wine rack can be a smart finishing touch

The double-L galley ahown here gives a visually interesting route through the boat but does take up space. This one also has a small, but very useful breakfast bar created by extending the worktop's forward edge

Fitting a shallow cupboard into the space under the gunwale can provide useful extra stowage room

Boat galleys have certainly changed. Not so long ago the average boater would have been perfectly content to set off for a week on the cut with a little two-burner gas cooker, a Paloma instant gas water heater and a 12v or gas fridge.

Not any more: in one of today's new boats you're likely find a galley as fully equipped as the kitchen you left behind at home: four burner gas hob, oven and grill, microwave, fridge, freezer, fancy stowage cupboards and gleaming granite worktops. Many are worthy of a feature in *25 Beautiful Kitchens* magazine.

But where your home kitchen designer is planning a space that is probably around 15ft by 12ft, the narrowboat galley planner has to work with something that's rarely more than 10ft long and never more than about 6ft 6in wide. It's quite a challenge and designers have come up with many different solutions.

As we have said earlier in the book, the galley is

very often the area in which the boat's line of movement changes. There is generally a side corridor past the cabin and a central route through the saloon: in the galley the two often meet.

GALLEY LAYOUTS

There are three basic galley layouts and a number of variations. The first, and simplest, is the straight-through, central corridor design. Galley units (and this means 'units' in the broadest terms, including sinks, cookers and fridges) sit either side of the boat and the cook (or cooks) work in the middle. The advantages are cheapness and simplicity – two straight rows of cupboards (with sink and cooker opposite each other) is easy to build and can be covered with standard-sized worktops. There are no hidden corners or hard-to-reach cupboards either, so it is an efficient system, too, packing the most units into the shortest length of boat.

The big disadvantage is that the cook is working

in the boat's main corridor and probably having to move hot pots and pans from side to side in it.

The U-shaped galley avoids this by separating the working zone from the corridor, which makes it well worth considering in a busy family boat. The cook has his/her own space and everything is readily to hand in a boating version of the compact 'working triangle' that kitchen design books enthuse over. It also links well with a dinette that can be built on to its forward edge.

The downside is that the galley needs to be quite long to give the cook room to move inside the 'U; longer still to accommodate the same amount of units as a central aisle design. Also the cupboard spaces in each corner are 'lost' and very hard to access. There are clever carousel and pull-out internal racks to get over this problem but, even these may not offer a complete solution. In the most compact form of the U-galley, the sink sits against the hull side with the fridge and cooker facing each

The U-shaped galley is a good all-round solution but its does leave dead corners at either end that have to be considered carefully at the planning stage

The rear galley layout has advantages when the steerer wants a quick cup of tea

A Welsh dresser is a good looking and useful piece of boat furniture

Washing machine, drier and freezer are best stored in a separate small utility area of the boat

This pull-out ironing board is an ingenious space-saver on a live-aboard boat

Clever 'magic corner' racking devices can be used to allow access into those awkward corners

other on opposite arms of the U. The result is that the corner cupboard area between the sink plumbing and its adjacent appliance will be very tricky to access.

The third galley layout is the L or 'double L' arrangement. Here, as the name suggests, one part of the galley is arranged in an L-shape, with its longest side along the line of the boat and a foreshortened L (or short straight run) is built the opposite way round on the other side. The effect is to create a diagonal walkway through the galley. The chief advantage is one of style. The galley can be attractively designed, breaks up the long, narrow feel of the boat and, again, links easily to a dinette.

The downside is that it is not a compact layout. To achieve the same number of 'units' as the aisle galley, it needs to be longer. There are those 'lost' corners again, though there is more flexibility in positioning appliances, and the cook will be working across the corridor, though not in the direct line of traffic, as in the corridor galley. The cabinetry can be tricky, too, if the galley is heavily stylised (and the resulting worktops can be costly).

There are variations on all of these basic schemes and it is well worth looking at plenty of boats and photos before coming up with your final plan. (A common addition to the 'U' galley, for example, is a shallow cupboard built into the opposite under-gunwale space which can be surprisingly useful for storing cans and packets.)

APPLIANCES

It's easy to pooh pooh boaters who set out with their fridge-freezers and washing machines, but there are few things worse than a too-small and cluttered galley with not enough space to store the groceries you've just bought.

Every narrowboat galley will start off with the basics of a sink, refrigerator and cooker. Sinks are many and varied, from the expensive, moulded in to a Corian worktop, to the simplest stainless steel B&Q unit. Don't skimp by getting one that's too small for your pans. Taps are down to personal preference, a common addition these days is a separate tap supplying filtered drinking water.

Earlier fridges would run on either gas or 12v electricity and gas was widely preferred because the appliance could be used without draining batteries. Boats safety regs have all but ruled gas fridges out of new boats, so the choice now is of 12 or 24v electric or a mains 220AC unit. This latter is much cheaper to buy but consumes more battery power (via the inverter); the former is quite energy efficient but will eventually drain down batteries and must be properly installed with the correct sized cabling as it demands a heavy current load when starting.

Most boaters are happy with Propane gas for their cooking. Though cookers must be designed for bottle rather than domestic gas, they are domestic in size and style and available either as a single unit or as separate hob, grill and oven.

Gas is perfectly safe if correctly installed on the boat and there are strict guidelines for this, however, some boaters would prefer a gas-free boat and for them the cooking choices are either a diesel-powered cooker or electricity. Electric cookers are very heavy consumers of power and can only be considered if the boat is designed with a stand-alone secondary generator of 6kW plus to feed it. An AC engine alternator will not be up to the job. A microwave cooker could be run by an AC alternator or a properly sized inverter. (Finding space for the microwave can be tricky – usual solution is for it to be boxed in inside a convenient cupboard.)

Domestically, the best known diesel (or oil) fired cooker is the famous Aga. The Aga itself is not suitable for boat use since it runs continuously but modern Aga-style cookers can be installed. These can be switched on and off by timer or directly and can also heat the boat's hot water. Because of their weight they need to be installed on the boat's centreline for correct balancing.

Other appliances such as freezers and washing machines can also go in the galley, though they eat up space and are probably better tucked away in a small utility area – perhaps at the stern of the boat where coats and boots can also go.

STORAGE

Once you have placed the cooker, fridge and sink in your galley you find that floor space is rapidly being used up and storage space running out. What is left is probably used to store pots, pans and crockery, and food storage is what suffers.

One solution is to have wall cupboards, though these can close the space in and make the galley feel crowded. Another popular, and very space-efficient solution is the full height, pull-out larder cupboard. Being deep but narrow it can be accommodated without too much difficulty, often between galley and bathroom where a certain amount of 'cheating' can be done to pinch a piece of bathroom wall space if necessary. Some builders make a virtue out of a necessity and create an arched opening from the galley, with a pull-out larder on one side and shelving opposite.

A Welsh dresser is another homely and practical feature that is popular among 'cottage style' boat fitters. An alternative is a transverse room divider unit placed across the front of the galley – but beware, should you come to a sudden stop unsecured items can come tumbling off so you will need 'fiddle rails' to prevent that! (For the same reason, try to specify 'positive closing' runners for drawers, which will prevent them flying open in the event of a bump.)

The more you look at boats and pictures of boats, the more clever storage details you will find which you may be able to incoporate into your new boat – clever wine racks are a favourite. (One of the best we have seen was an underfloor stowage area which kept the owner's white wine nicely chilled in the cool of the bilges!)

Whatever you do in your design, don't forget the wastebin. Too many lovely galleys are spoiled by having an old plastic bag wrapped round a door handle to hold the rubbish!

Keeping the wine cool: this ingenious wine cabinet is built into the under-floor space

And whatever you do, don't forget the rubbish bin

The through galley is simple and takes up minimum length of the boat but the cook will be working in the main gangway through it

The bathroom

The smallest room has to be particularly space-efficient on a narrowboat and there are a number of clever ways of achieving this goal as we explain in this section

You'd scarcely know that this luxurious bathroom with its full length, free-standing bath and stylish fittings was actually in a narrowboat, but it is

The smallest room certainly doesn't deserve the smallest attention when it comes to narrowboat planning. In fact, it demands careful design to achieve the most comfort and, er, convenience for its users in what is usually a very compact space.

The bathroom generally sits near the centre of the boat. Here it can be accessed easily at night by those using either the main or secondary sleeping accommodation. However, this does mean that those on the boat have to get past it when moving around the boat during the day.

There are two ways of achieving this. The commonest way is to have the room to one side with a corridor running past. The alternative is the 'through' or 'cross' bathroom which, as the name suggests is across the full width of the boat and has a corridor running through it, closed off by doors at either end. There are pros and cons for each.

To leave sufficient space for a corridor, the side bathroom is restricted to around four feet wide while the room itself is usually no more than six feet long – about the minimum needed to allow space for basin, toilet and bath or shower.

That means there isn't a great deal of space for manoeuvre when it comes to positioning the bathroom fittings. Almost inevitably the basin and toilet will be along one wall with the bath or shower opposite. And there isn't a great amount of drying space in between them.

Incorporating the corridor means that the through bathroom is going to be about 50 per cent bigger than the side bathroom for any given length. This means the room itself can be made shorter to release space elsewhere in the boat or the extra space can be used to enable more flexibility in the internal layout and provide more room for drying. Or it can, quite simply, be used to make a style statement as you can see from the pictures here.

It's a tempting configuration, except that when the bathroom is in use, the route through the boat is closed off – something that is not practical on a busy craft. One way round this is to position the basin and toilet to one side of the gangway and bath or shower to the other, with the doors carefully positioned so that they can either close off the two areas separately or close across the corridor to create a through bathroom.

A second toilet is a very useful consideration in a family boat and can be very compact – the smallest we have seen is in one of the New Boat Company's Aqualine craft. Here the front and side walls actually slide forwards to provide the user with adequate space inside the toilet, and slide back up against the toilet when the room is not in use – the smallest room indeed!

A second toilet can bring plumbing complications, especially if it is remote from the rest of the boat's plumbing. However, the sensible option is to keep things simple and regard the second toilet as a fail-safe in case of problems elsewhere – a holding tank that can't be emptied or an electric toilet that has broken. The simple Porta Potti might be basic but it can't go wrong!

BATHROOM FITTINGS

In the past, bath and toilet fittings for boats tended to come from caravans because these were lighter, cheaper and more compact. Now tastes have changed, and so has the range of products available, and most bathroom fittings, with the exception of the necessarily specialised toilets are generally sourced from the domestic market.

One example of the way changing domestic tastes is reflected in boat fittings, is the widespread move away from baths to showers. Showers are very practical in boats; they take up less floorspace and use less water. In many bathrooms they can also be positioned so that off-the-shelf domestic cubicles can be used, at considerable savings in cost.

The 'wetroom' has become fashionable for home showering – dispensing with the cubicle altogether in favour of water resistant walls and a floor designed to channel water into a drain outlet. In boats, such an arrangement has long been in use since it enables good use of small spaces. Some boats have a lift-out floor panel; others an angled floor and either the walls can be tiled or a shower curtain used to limit splashing. The used water is channelled into a sump and pumped overboard via a bilge-type pump.

Before the re-emergence of showers, caravan-derived 'hip baths' were a traditional fitment, usually with a mixer-type shower. It's easy to see why these not especially comfortable items have lost ground but, for those who do want a bath, it's worth pointing out that full length baths and narrowboats need not be incompatible. The 5ft 6in standard bath can even be fitted in the typical 6ft bathroom. Shortcomings are that they do use a lot of water and, unless you are prepared to have a big bathroom, they don't leave much space for towels and drying yourself in the room.

The wide range of basins now available has helped the narrowboat bathroom planner greatly – circular and oval bowls can be fitted neatly in corners, for example, or placed on handy storage cabinets. Toilet choice is limited only by your budget: from the simple plastic cassette to porcelain items indistinguishable from those at home.

A heated towel rail is always useful to keep towels (and the room) warm, and it's a good idea to run it from the hot water calorifier rather than through the central heating so that it is warm even when the heating is off. (We know of one boat where the supply pipe was run behind the bathroom mirror to keep this mist-free. Neat!)

Finally, don't forget ventilation, for reasons of both hygiene and to remove moisture: various systems are available from combined light-cum-fan units to solar powered extractor fans.

This compact bath with a shower over is a familiar narrowboat installation

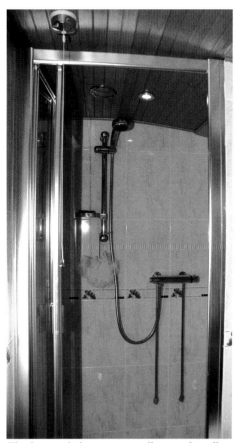

The shower cubicle is very space efficient and an off-the-shelf domestic item can often be fitted

A second toilet is very useful in a big boat: this compact one is fitted in a discreet corner of the boat

The popular bowl-style of this domestic basin is easily adapted for use in a narrowboat

Not every narrowboat toilet is quite as extraordinary looking as this one found in a Louis and Joshua boat

The floor of this wetroom style shower room slopes down to a central drain channel

This Aqualine boat has a stylishly arranged modern basin and toilet in a fitted vanity unit

The cabin

The modern narrowboat cabin can offer all the comforts of home – but only if it is carefully planned. We examine the options available in making night-time comfortable

This main cabin is at the front of the boat and features a cross-double bed that extends full-width across the cabin and has storage cabinets above the head end

A mattress extension and pull-out bed base allow the bed's width to be increased to full double size

The standard lengthways double bed is restricted to four feet in width to allow a gangway alongside

Boats and beds don't traditionally go well together. From the hammocks of Nelson's navy to the cramped 'bed 'ole' of the narrowboat boatman's cabin, getting a good night's sleep has always been secondary to having enough room for the main business of the day – whether it be fighting or cargo carrying.

A modern 57ft long cruising narrowboat ought, though, to be able to find enough room somewhere for a comfortable 6ft 6in long double bed – but, oddly, creating a full-sized double bed is still a bit of a problem for the narrowboat builder.

It's easy to see why. If we assume that boat's owners don't want to have to assemble a futon or convert a bed-settee each night, then they will most likely want a fixed double bed for the master cabin.

If the bed is placed lengthways in the boat then it will need a gangway past – which means a maximum width of about four feet. That's six inches less than the standard double – and remember that

one occupant will be hard up against the cabin side, making it feel smaller still. (The cabin wall-side occupant will also have to clamber over the other should he or she need to make a night time visit to the loo or such like.)

The solution to this is a bed extension to take it up to 4ft 6in or, more usually, five feet wide. This can be either a lift-up flap on the outside edge of the bed, a slide out extension or even a means by which the whole bed slides out from the wall. In all cases an infilling mattress section is slotted into place between the hull and the main mattress. It sounds fiddly but in these days of duvets and fitted sheets, just a matter of seconds' work.

The alternative arrangement is the 'cross-double' which provides adequate width (as much as you like, in fact, as the boat runs across the bed.) It is also a little easier for the occupant on the far side of the bed from the bathroom to get to it without disturbing the other sleeper. However, to facilitate the gangway

through in daytime, at least part of the bed must be de-mountable in some fashion. Again, this can be achieved by a mattress extension supported on a pull-out section or, more usually, by a flap – and we know of at least one such flap that is electrically operated.

Both systems have their devotees: the cross bed generally takes up less room in the boat since few people will want more than the regulation five feet of a king size bed. It also doesn't leave one sleeper trapped against the cabin side at night! In return it possibly takes fractionally more making up, offers a bit less potential under-bed storage and the cabin doors must be designed to allow access out of the room even with the bed folded out, for safety reasons.

That's the captain and first mate sorted out – what about the rest of the crew? Unless you are solitary travellers or isolationist live-aboarders there will almost certainly be times when you want friends and family to stay.

A diminishing number of new narrowboats seem to be built with multiple fixed berths, reflecting the change in market tastes away from family users towards older buyers. Fixed berths eat into valuable cabin space and as a result possibly affect your resale potential so unless you really need them, it's probably worth looking at the various convertible options.

For those who do want extra fixed berths – and that generally means family buyers – the commonest route is for bunk beds. A pair of bunks can be squeezed either side of a central corridor in a narrowboat, though the top pair will necessarily be narrow because of the narrowing of the cabin sides above the gunwales and only suitable for young children.

For someone wanting two bunks, the best choice is to place them to one side of the boat, where they can be made full single bed width and still allow a good corridor alongside.

The most popular convertible additional bed is the dinette. The four-seater Pullman dinette, featuring a bench seat either side of a table is the same length and width as a double bed and can be easily converted into one. The table top drops down onto lips on the leading edges of the benches and the seat back cushions form the infill mattress. Bedding is generally stowed inside one of the seat benches. To make things a bit more private, a curtain can often be arranged to pull across the boat behind the dinette.

An alternative conversion is based around a fixed sofa in the saloon, often L-shaped which again can be extended or linked with a dining table top to form a second double bed.

This L-shaped dinette sofa can easily be extended to provide a second double berth at night

THE BACK CABIN

The traditional back cabin provided accommodation for the boatman and his family in working narrowboats. It is unlikely to become so crowded in today's replica boats, but can still provide very practical secondary sleeping space.

The boatman's cabin is typically laid out with a long bench to one side, with a stove opposite and then a large built-in structure. This holds a fold-down table and, beyond it, a wide fold-down flap that drops down to meet a section of the bench and form a cross double (well, just about a double) bed, with its bedding contained in the bed cupboard or 'bed 'ole'. In the working boat the bench would have a dividing curtain alongside the bed, separating off the remainder of the bench on which could slip the boatman's children.

Various smaller cupboards and niches – all built to very precise styles if you are a traditionalist – complete the cabin, which is, of course, finished in intricate paintwork and 'scumbling'.

Today, the main cross bed can be a useful secondary double bed and the cabin's dimensions can be tailored a little to create a useful bed of about four feet wide. The back cabin is also handy as a day cabin, allowing other people on the boat to be close to the steerer – and out of the rain on a wet day.

The versatility of the back cabin idea means that it has been adopted by many builders in various non-traditional ways. The simplest, and one of the most effective, is a simple bench down either side of the boat that can be used either for seating or as single berths.

This versatile Sea Otter interior has a pair of sofas facing each other that can be used as single berths or converted to form a double bed

This room is a saloon during the day with a sofa each side and converts to a double cabin with a full-width bed at night, using a pull-out extension between them

Unusually, the space under the end of this cross-bed is used to hide a filing cabinet

STORAGE

No-one goes off on a canal boat trip loaded with Gucci suitcases but, during an English summer, you still need clothes for just about every sort of weather. And that means you will need plenty of space on the boat in which to store it.

So be careful: in the pursuit of space for eating or relaxing elsewhere, it is easy to cut back on storage areas but once omitted, they can rarely be restored. Wardrobes are the obvious starting point: a single wardrobe per person incorporating half-height hanging space with shelves above is the norm. A familiar location for these would be across the boat at the bulkhead between cabin and bathroom – though space has to be left to access them. Alternatively they are built along the length of the boat which can allow deeper cupboard space but is less space efficient.

Wardrobes are generally complemented by overbed cupboards – often nicely shaped around

porthole windows. Reading lights are usually fitted under these and switches for main room lights and heating controls can usefully be put here, too, so they can be used from the comfort of the bed.

The underbed space is also very useful for storage, though access can be tricky – simplest way is down through the top or via a lift-off front panel but the tidiest (albeit costliest) way is to have underbed drawers. Problem here is that you can't pull out a full depth four feet drawer in a two feet wide corridor: a common solution is to use shallower front drawer linked to another behind it – the first is pulled out and removed to reveal the second.

Finally, don't forget that the cabin should be a place of comfort and retreat after the rigours of a hard day on the cut. Four poster beds can sometimes be found on narrowboats and a bed curtain offers similar privacy but whatever your choice of design, always make the furnishings warm and relaxing.

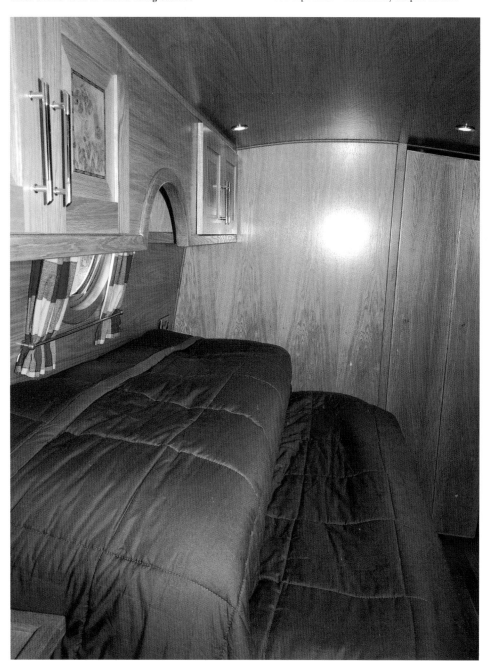

The mattress pull-out extension of a cross-double bed can clearly be seen here. The cross-bed takes up less length in the boat since few people will want more than the regulation 5ft wide bed but does demand making up at night

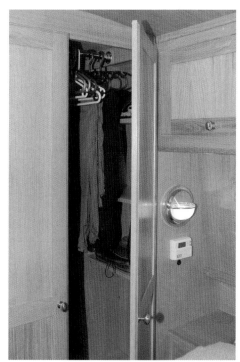

A good amount of wardrobe and clothes cupboard space is needed on any narrowboat

The space under this raised-up captain's bed provides a massive amount of storage

NARROWBOAT EQUIPMENT

Over 14,000 products available online at www.aquafax.co.uk

Victron Inverters & Chargers

Phoenix Easyplus

- 12 Volt 1600VA sine wave inverter
- 70A charger incl. 4A trickle charge for start battery
- Unique PowerAssist© technology
- 4 stage adaptive charge technology for quick and accurate battery charging
- RCD (30mA/16A) on AC output
- Two AC output sockets protected by 16A automatic circuit breakers for optimum safety
- No-break system

Spinflo Ovens, Cookers & Hobs

Mk3 Caprice

SPINFLO

- Combination oven, grill and hob
- 4 cooking burners & one grill & one oven burner
- Possibility to include electric hot plate
- Separate grill
- Hot inside, max 60°C outside
- Many different materials and finishes possible (glass, knobs, handles)
- Reliable, high quality product
- Easy to install

Aarrow Fires

Acorn Fire

- Burns wood, peat & solid fuel
- Airwash system for clean glass
- Patented multifuel grate
- Top or rear fitting 4" flue
- Floor fixing kit available as optional extra
- 3 year warranty on main body
- 0.5 - 4.5 kW heat output

Albion Marine Calorifiers

Foam Moulded Marine Calorifiers

Albion *HEATING WATER FOR YOU*

- Supplied with mixer valve assembly
- 750W 1¼" BSP heating element
- 3.5 bar relief valve setting
- 3.0 bar max working pressure
- ½" male BSP connections
- Twin Coil

Johnson Pumps

Viking Power 16

- Specifically designed to pump wastewater
- Easy to install, even in tight spaces
- Easy, low cost maintenance
- Non-choke valves - no filters required
- Self-priming up to 3m (9.8ft)
- KlickTite™ connectors standard
- Low power consumption

BCS Bow Thrusters

Electric Bow Thrusters

- Easy installation with modern proven design
- New control panel with built-in motor protection
- Corrosion free propeller with anode protection on bronze leg
- Available in 12 or 24 volt
- Quiet operation
- Hydraulic option available on 6hp model

Tecma Toilets

Silence Toilet

TECMA

- Push button control operation
- Complete automatic flushing cycle
- Low water consumption
- Whisper quiet during operation
- Easy clean Vitreous - China bowl
- Macerator incorporated in bowl base
- Easy to install

Blue Sea Electricals

AC Voltmeter/ Ammeter Panel

BLUE SEA SYSTEMS

- Matches all full AC size circuit breaker panels
- Marked to ABYC Standards

BC Electrical Techniques

Galvanic Isolator

- With indicator
- For use with 120/240V 50//60Hz 16A supplies
- Will block galvanic currents in the shore earth connection up to 1.1V
- Above 1.1V current is allowed to pass maintaining the safety earth connection

Aquafax

Marine and Industrial Equipment Specialists

Visit our website:
www.aquafax.co.uk

For further information and details of stockists contact:

Aquafax Limited (Middlewich), Unit 11, Valley Court, Sanderson Way, Middlewich, Cheshire CW10 0GF Tel: (01606) 841111 Fax: (01606) 841188 E-mail: middlewich@aquafax.co.uk

The shell

The shell is the cornerstone of a narrowboat. Its design underwater determines the boat's performance and its details above the water determine its appeal and value

The narrowboat shell is a relatively simple structure in theory – a rectangular box with shaped underwater sections at front and rear but quality detail design and finishing enable the builder to show off his skills

Stern swim in this quality shell ends in taper. Depth of swim is height from base plate to counter above prop

A standard narrowboat hull is essentially a rectangular box with a point at the bow, a tapered stern (the 'swim') and a flat bottom. The style and design of the bow and the stern are mainly what sets boats apart in terms of looks and performance. The cabin sides and roof complete the structure and together with the hull are known collectively as the 'shell'.

One of the most fundamental shell specifications is the steel thickness. Typically this is quoted as '10/6/4' this being the steel thickness in millimetres of the base plate (10mm), the hull sides (6mm) and the cabin sides and roof (4mm). Base plate thickness is sometimes increased to 12 or 15mm, but there is not much evidence that this is necessary as most corrosion takes place at or near the waterline. However the thicker base plate will slightly reduce the weight of added ballast needed to float the boat with sufficient stability. The base plate, hull and cabin sides and roof are all internally braced to stiffen the plates and to strengthen the complete shell.

A new boat's shell also has to be built to conform to the Recreational Craft Directive standards and marked as such.

THE HULL

A narrowboat hull is essentially a 'displacement hull', as opposed to a 'planing hull' (power boats), or 'semi-planing' hull (fast sailing boats). Basically this means that it has to move all of the water past the hull in order to move forward. The majority of ships and boats used to carry both people and cargo are displacement hulls so narrowboaters should not feel too inferior about the relative simplicity of their hulls! Though most hulls are flat-bottomed it's worth mentioning that some (including the aluminium Sea Otter) have a shallow vee-section which can work better on very shallow canals.

The basics of hydrodynamics in narrowboat hull design are important in relation to draft, efficiency of water movement past the propeller, tendency to create wash, and compatibility with propeller options.

A deep drafted boat will in theory be more efficient because the propeller can draw more water past itself but it is only really a sensible option if the boat is to spend the majority of its life on rivers or the deeper commercial river/canal network in Yorkshire. Even the legal 4mph limit is very often not achievable due to limited depths on many canals.

Excessive boat and propeller speed is in any case counter productive on most inland waterways because the combination of 'squat' (slight tendency to suck down at the stern), and draw down of water coming past the boat reduce the effective depth for navigation.

THE SWIM

The stern 'swim' is the tapered hull section below the water line at the stern which allows the water flowing past the boat to be sucked into the propeller. The design and construction of the stern swim is one of the most critical aspects in the navigational performance of all boats and none less so with narrowboats.

Within reason, the longer the swim, the more efficient the propeller will be. In practice the length is limited by a combination of cost, as it is one of the more expensive parts of the hull to make, and practicalities such as loss of inside cabin space due to the narrowing hull section.

Inevitably on longer boats it tends to be more generous, typically about 12ft (3.7m) or more from the start of the taper to the stern post. Absolute minimum swim length for shorter boats is about 8ft (2.4m). The taper is not constant but should ideally be 'S' shaped in plan view so that the water is presented as near as possible at 90 degrees to the propeller blades. In practice most begin with a gentle curl and terminate in a straight taper at the stern post.

The swim terminates in a stern post in which the stern tube carrying the propeller shaft is mounted. Ideally this should be made as a sharp vertical tapered joint but some builders prefer to terminate it as a flat vertical plate which makes it easier to weld the stern tube into.

The depth of the swim is the height from the hull base plate to the underside of the 'counter' – the horizontal flat plate which supports the rear deck overhanging the swim section. Deep drafted boats can afford to have a deep swim which also allows a bigger propeller.

Minimum clearance between the tips of the propeller blades and the underside of the swim should be 2in (50mm) with the same clearance to the 'skeg' at the bottom. Therefore the maximum propeller diameter is limited to 4ins (100mm) less than the swim depth. The efficiency of a combination of long, deep swim and largish propeller compared to a shallow short swim and small propeller make a huge difference to the efficiency of propulsion. Also a deep swim makes reversing a little more controllable as it gives better directional stability.

THE RUDDER

The rudder and tiller bar are a very simple and effective method of steering a narrowboat. The tiller bar is usually a swan-necked solid round steel bar which extends through the back deck, down through the diesel tank and through the counter where it connects with the rudder itself.

The rudder is a simple flat plate welded or bolted to the lower part of the tiller bar, (sometimes called the 'stock'). The bottom of the stock is located in a simple cup bearing which is supported by the 'skeg', a substantial beam welded underneath the base plate and extends backwards under the stern post. Hence the skeg is actually the deepest part of the hull and is the part most likely to drag on underwater obstructions such as debris in bridge holes or lock sills.

There are several important design features which should be built in but which do not significantly add to the cost. Firstly, the tiller post should be angled backwards slightly so that the overhanging weight of the rudder plate causes the rudder and tiller to fall to the centre ('neutral steering' as with road vehicles).

Secondly, the rudder blade should be adequately balanced to partially counteract the throw of water off the propeller. This is achieved by having a proportion of the blade forward of the tiller pin pivot point in the skeg. This is particularly significant with bigger propellers. Thirdly, it is sensible to make contingency for re-fitting the tiller and rudder should the assembly become unshipped on an obstruction, (typically a lock sill on descending a lock with the stern too close to the upper sill!).

Lastly, the larger the blade, the better the steering response, but do ensure that there is sufficient length of stern fendering to reduce the risk of the blade fouling on lock gates or sills.

THE BOW

Below the wate,r the design of the bow swim is less critical in terms of navigational performance

The semi-trad stern design shown here preserves the classic narrowboat look whilst providing extra space that allows three or four extra crew members to keep the steerer company in the stern

than the stern swim. So long as there is reasonable transition from the stem post to full hull width over a minimum of approximately 8ft (2.4m) the boat will perform satisfactorily.

In terms of usable hull space the shorter this section the better, but aesthetics do come into it, and there is no denying that a long sweeping bow is more graceful and elegant than a short stubby one. Many shell builders also sweep the base plate upwards to the bow thus improving the hydrodynamic performance of the bow to cut through water more efficiently. However this is only likely to significantly improve the overall

performance on very deep and wide navigations.

The part of the bow which is visible and the front deck come in several different styles and designs such as 'Replica', 'Josher' or 'Tug' style.

Replica is a working boat style, mainly copying front deck and cabin details. It usually includes lots of imitation rivets to copy early methods of joining plates when motorised working boats were first built. This detailing can transform the appearance of a boat but it does add significantly to the construction costs.

Josher is a particular style of replica hull with an elegant double curve shape formed of steel strips, which can also include an extra small cabin in front of the bow deck called the 'Potter's Cabin'. Apparently this is where boat children were often consigned to sleep in early working boats! To fully replicate this design would normally include replica rivet details.

Tug Style is a replica of canal tug boats. Typically these are shorter than replica carrying boats and have a notably long low front deck, level with the gunwales (sometimes a slide-away or fixed bed is fitted under here). They usually appear to float lower and often are deep drafted, have high cabin sides and low hull sides giving a squat and compact appearance. Tug style, Josher and other replica design boats are often fitted with original or replica vintage marine engines to complete the reproduction effect.

STERN DECK AND BACK CABIN

Narrowboats have three styles of rear deck: Traditional ('Trad'), Cruiser, and Semi Trad.

Hull details like these on a Tim Tyler shell are what mark out a top quality hull

This large open cruiser stern provides ample space for socialising which makes it ideal for holiday hire, family and other busy boats. Downside is that engine compartment is underfoot so it can be noisy and is also prone to ingress of water from rain

Traditional as the name suggests, is a copy of the back end of traditional working boats. It offers only a small space for the steerer to stand with safety, which can be a disadvantage when cruising with family or friends. A big advantage of a trad stern is that when closed up the back cabin doors give total protection against the elements and don't require any extra winter protection.

The **Cruiser** stern became popular on hire boats because it offers large open deck space usually with the engine underneath. It is eminently more sociable when cruising with family and friends as there is space for up to 6-8 people whilst cruising. Also the engine gearbox and weed hatch are all very quickly and easily accessible by lifting the deck panels.

Disadvantages include engine noise and exposure of the rear deck and engine to weather and winter elements – an efficient drainage system is vital to prevent the engine bilges from filling with rainwater.

The **Semi Trad** is, as the name suggests, a cross between the full trad and cruiser style stern. Visually it has the look of the traditional boat, which many prefer, but inside the final 4-5ft of the sides there will be provision for extra seating thus creating a much more sociable area around the steerer, although with not as much space as a full cruiser stern. Inevitably the semi trad is a compromise including some of the pros and cons of both the other styles, but it does offer a good alternative option.

WINDOWS

There are two main options for windows in a narrowboat, either portholes or 'bus type' windows. Arguably portholes are more secure than bus windows since they are likely to be too small for an intruder to get through.

Fully traditional and replica boats look more original with portholes, however they let in a lot less light than the bigger bus type windows. This can be overcome by fitting opening roof windows which are also very efficient overhead ventilators for hot weather. Commonly called 'Houdini hatches', they can also be used as an emergency escape route. They give a softer overhead light than side windows and a lot less shadows and less direct sunlight into the cabin.

Side hatches also allow light and air into the boat – as well as an opportunity to feed the swans! The addition of lightweight sliding or hinged glazed inner doors means they can stay open when the weather's bad outside.

Bus windows are so called because they often resemble the old style of top hopper opening windows that used to be fitted to buses, though there are other variations including slide opening

Double sweep of a Josher bow is good looking but costly to construct, being formed from shaped strips of steel

and many shapes and sizes. They provide much more visibility to outside which may not always be a good thing (many boats with windows in public areas have portholes in the cabin and bathroom). One downside of windows is the number and cost of individual curtains required, whereas portholes can be furnished with very simple curtains or even push-in pads.

Windows are a common area for rain water leakage if they are not well designed or fitted properly. This is an area where it is particularly well worth paying for a good design and getting good advice on fixing and sealing.

HAND RAILS

Unless the boat does not have gunwales at all it is essential to have a hand rail or similar as a grab rail when walking along the gunwales. New traditional style boats tend to have an upstand hand grab integrally formed as an upward extension to the top of the cabin sides. These give a cleaner impression of the line and form of the cabin sides compared to a separate handrail.

Cruiser-style boats often opt for a conventional handrail fixed 2-3in inside the top cabin edge. Some experienced hire boat companies regard the handrail as safer than the upstand type as the user can fully grasp the rail with all fingers and thumb should they slip on the gunwales, which is not at all uncommon even with experienced boaters. Upstand handrails are not exclusively traditional since many of the original working boats had conventional handrails. As ever the choice is a compromise between appearance and effectiveness.

HULL DETAILS

It's the details that can make the difference between a plain boat and a pretty one. 'Recessed' side panels to carry the boat's name are popular and you can find nicely detailed hand rail ends, locker hinges and even deck drain holes.

INSULATION

It is essential to install thermal insulation in a narrowboat shell before or during fitting out, and there are a number of options:

Sprayed Urethane Foam is currently the most popular option but it also the most expensive as it has to be applied by a specialist contractor. It will also need a certain amount of tedious trimming back of excessive foam before lining-out begins. It does have the huge advantage of virtually eliminating condensation on the inside of the hull since it sticks hard to the steel and also seals totally against the irregular shapes and curves of the shell.

However avoid, or take extra care, when welding to the hull after the foam is on as, although it should be specified to 'BS 476 pt7 Class I Spread

The traditional or 'trad' stern is derived from that of the old working narrow boats, though they wouldn't have enjoyed the modern seats. Space is limited and it will only take one or two people but space in the cabin is maximised

All the narrowboat shell builder's skills can be seen in the roof details of this Barry Hawkins replica working boat: the false rivets, intricte handrails and cabin roof break-line. A visual delight – but it does come at a price

Angled tiller bar ensures balanced rudder

Dog box is another traditional detail to let light in boat

A short bow swim like this is not ideal for handling

of Flame Rating', it can nevertheless catch fire if there is enough heat and oxygen, or a direct flame present. Gas cutting equipment should definitely never be used on a sprayed foam hull.

Thinsulate, produced by 3M, is the main alternative to spray foam on new craft and you'll find staunch advocates of both products. Thinsulate is well known as an insulation material in clothing but is becoming increasingly popular in boats because it offers competitive thermal insulation as well as acoustic insulation and is particularly easy to apply. It is a multi-layer sheet material which is easily cut and then spray-glued to the hull.

Expanded Polystyrene and **Polystyrene foam** (*'Styrofoam'*) boards are an older and cheaper alternative but will need about 50mm (2in) to get a similar 'U' value of 0.2. The foam boards are slightly denser and therefore give slightly better insulation than expanded polystyrene. Cable runs must be in conduit as polystyrene has a chemical reaction with most types of cable sheathing, making them dangerously brittle. The boards will have a significant labour element in fixing them to the steel and a lot of cutting and trimming to get a good fit to the shell.

Glass fibre or Rockwool is the cheapest insulation material and a slightly better insulator than both expanded and foamed polystyrene but not as good as polyurethane. The main advantage is low cost but the serious disadvantage is that the material offers virtually no resistance to moisture, and may even increase rate of rust formation on steel. It can also be very irritating to work with and you will require gloves and a face mask.

BALLAST
A steel narrowboat hull has to be ballasted to increase stability and to achieve sufficient draft for effective operation of the propeller. A number of different ballasting materials are in use, but the most common are concrete paving slabs. Ideally these can be sized to fit exactly between the steel joists on the base plate. More drastic methods include pouring wet concrete into the gaps between the joists, or using loose sand.

The positioning and amount of ballast is a mixture of guesswork and experience since it depends on the weight of the fitting out equipment, the weight of the engine, size of water, fuel and sewage tanks etc. The problem being that by the time the boat fit out is complete the under floor ballast is often no longer accessible! If using paving slabs it is good practice to support them on non corrosive spacers to reduce moisture formation and corrosion on the steel base plate, old plastic water hose is ideal. (The interior of the hull is often waxoyl treated as well as primed before ballast is installed to prevent dampness causing corrosion.

Additional moveable ballast is also useful to allow for subsequent alterations to the fit out, and to accommodate changes in boat trim whilst navigating, e.g. full to empty tanks, extra crew etc. Typically additional ballast is items of solid scrap steel such as old railway line or sash window weights.

PAINTING AND BLACKING
Initially the entire shell is usually primed in a base coat of red oxide by the boat builder. Prior to this it is worth considering grit blasting to remove surface corrosion and mill scale. Though quite costly (upwards of £750), grit blasting will ensure a better key for the primer and longer paint life and should be followed by immediate coating with a quality epoxy primer.

This long and elegant S-shaped rear swim optimises the performance of the propellor by directing the flow of water past the boat to meet the prop at ninety degrees. The longer the swim, the more efficient the prop will be

Side hatches like these let light and air into the boat and are commonly located in the galley area or alongside the engine rooms of vintage-powered boats. An internal window can be arranged to keep the draughts out if needs be

The superstructure (i.e. cabin roof and sides, decks, doors etc) should be finished with a good quality marine grade enamel paint. Bear in mind that the boat will probably have to live outside in all weathers for about ten years before a re-paint and therefore good quality paints are essential. Some colours, e.g. red, fade badly in strong sunlight due to ultra violet degradation and therefore it is wise to limit how much of these colours are in the paint scheme.

The hull is normally finished in black bitumen which is a semi-setting heavy tar based paint. As a general rule the hull should be scraped, cleaned

(pressure washing is the best way) and re-painted every 2-3 years. It should also be routinely touched-up after the inevitable scrapes to avoid corrosion.

Alternative hull paints include much higher spec paints, e.g. two pack paints, and galvanitic surface treatments such as those used on North Sea oil platforms which provide improved protection against local corrosion caused by paint scrapes and enable longer intervals between re-blacking. Most of the higher spec hull paints cannot be over painted on bitumen, in fact virtually nothing can, so it is important to decide from the start what type of paint system to go for.

Don't envy beauty.
Apply it.

Which beauty treatment should you choose?

Toplac is our premium quality silicone-alkyd enamel. Deep, very long-lasting gloss, with the best quality UV stabilisers.

Brightside® is our superior quality one-pack polyurethane quick-drying enamel. It is the only yacht finish in the world that contains Teflon®, producing a hard, tough, abrasion resistant and easy to clean surface.

Toplac and Brightside are ideal for retaining the youthful glamour of boats made of steel, GRP, aluminium and wood.

Show Your True Colour

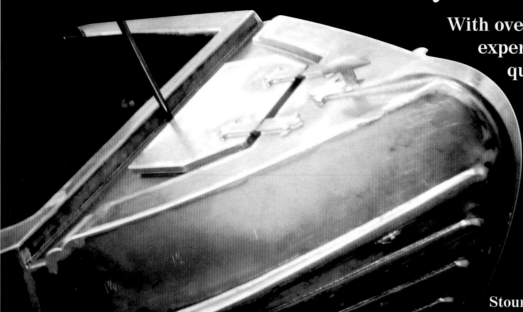

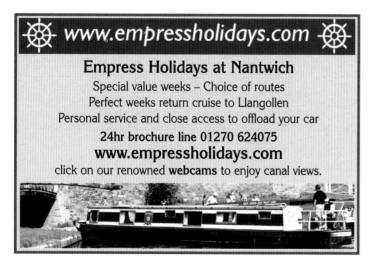

The Engine

There might be a four mph speed limit on our canals but the right choice of engine is still important in your boat

Beta 'Greenline' 43, above, is probably the most commonly seen current narrowboat engine

A majestic fully restored Gardner 2L2 standing proudly in its engine room

In the past a single horse was able to pull a loaded narrowboat with relative ease, which goes to show that horsepower is not the main criterion when it comes to selecting a canal boat engine.

As anyone who has tried to do the job of the poor old boat horse will appreciate, the hardest thing is to start a boat moving; once it is slipping through the water, keeping it moving at the steady walking pace that is canal speed is not too demanding.

Torque – turning power – (or 'grunt' if you want the technical term!) is what counts in a boat, whereas sheer power and a good power to weight ratio are the performance factors in cars.

Power boat engines and small outboards for light craft will be of the light, high revving type, and mostly petrol, but elsewhere larger slow revving engines, usually diesel, are better because they deliver – these are the designs that deliver the necessary pull.

MARINE DIESELS

For canal boats diesels can be categorised into three types; traditional/vintage specialist marine engines, industrial/agricultural marine conversion and variations, and modern high-speed automotive diesels adapted for marine use.

Traditional and vintage marine diesels have a very evocative and satisfying sound and feel in a traditional boat which can never be imitated or replaced by more modern engines. They are typically fitted to restored and replica working boats with deep drafts and large propellers, and displayed on view in engine rooms.

Makes include Lister, National, Russell Newberry, Gardner, Sabb, Kelvin and Bolinder, but there are many more and some quite obscure makes from abroad. All are typically very high capacity, slow revving, long stroke engines with very large flywheels and huge torque.

The best of these engines are now rare and highly sought after, so many now on canal boats will actually have been rescued from commercial vehicle or industrial applications.

Relative to other types of marine engine, the traditional engine will be very slow revving, (300 –1500 rpm), and in horsepower terms not particularly powerful. It is the huge torque which is so valuable and the sheer momentum of the large flywheel which will get a large propeller spinning quickly, and can slow down a heavy boat quickly when in reverse.

Industrial/agricultural conversions are specially marinised versions of light industrial and agricultural power units, typically around 1.5 to 3 litres capacity, revving at 600 –2500rpm, and with adequate torque for most boats.

Until the introduction of modern high-speed diesels over the last 10-15 years, this type of engine powered nearly all new build canal boats and river cruisers. Makes include Perkins, Lister, Beta, BMC (derivatives and re-worked engines), Ford, Mitsubishi (as Vetus) and many others.

In some respects these engines are still traditional in that they are typically overhead valve rather than overhead cam, and will have gear or chain driven camshafts as opposed to a cam belt.

Automotive Marine Diesel conversions are typically 1 – 2 litres capacity and revving at 900-3000rpm in marine mode. Essentially these engines are best suited to smaller narrowboats and river cruisers with smaller propellers and where high torque is not required.

Many modern diesels now have an overhead camshaft which has a rubber cam belt drive from the crankshaft. Some traditional canal boat engineers are nervous about the serviceability of this type of engine including the risk of cam belt failure especially if the engine is subject to excessive load or torque at slow engine speeds.

Therefore, it is essential that these engines are paired with a suitable gearbox which allows a reasonably high engine speed to be maintained without excessive propeller speed. This type of engine should be run at higher speeds to ensure good circulation of the engine oil otherwise "sludging", (accumulation of combustion by-products), may occur in the sump.

The majority of industrially-derived marine diesels are 'direct injection' which means fuel is injected straight into the combustion chamber. Newer designs are following the trend started in automotive diesels in being 'indirectly injection' with fuel going into a small pre-chamber. These tend to be sweeter and quieter running than the older designs. This could be an important factor particularly for a cruiser or semi-trad-style boat.

The BMC diesel was once the stalwart marine diesel but has now been superceded by more modern units

This version of the Beta Greenline 43 is fully encapsulated to minimise noise

This John Deere is mounted sideways and drives the prop and bow thrusters by a hydraulic drive system

The traditional stern gland is topped up with grease daily by the manual greaser seen here

The rugged Lister Canalstar has been another reliable performer

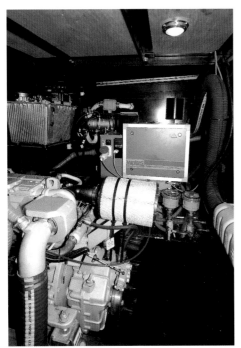

This is the impressive – and impressively complex – engine room of a Dutch barge

The 55hp version of the popular Isuzu range of marine diesels

A handsome restored Russell Newbury being installed in its engine room

ENGINE SIZE

In the main engine size is determined by the length and weight of the boat, the size of propeller and the type of use, i.e. will the boat be primarily used on rivers or canals? There is no hard and fast rule, but for canal use, up to say 60ft (18m), about 0.6hp/ft (1.5kw/m) seems to be adequate.

For extensive river use it is probably best to allow another 5-10hp or so over and above the minimum needed for canals due to the likelihood of longer spells at higher speeds on river sections. Above 60ft the ratio is less meaningful since the importance of a high torque will take precedence over the horsepower.

It is also essential that the load from ancillary equipment is factored in. Many modern narrowboat engines are now driving two alternators (one for the starter battery, the other, larger unit to recharge several domestic batteries) and some drive a third, 220v AC alternator as well. All of these use up engine power when under load, as, of course, would hydraulic bow thrusters if fitted when these are used.

ENGINE MOUNTS

If at all possible all boat engines should be mounted to the hull on flexible mountings. These are specially designed blocks of rubber with the engine fixing bolts moulded into them, and they not only have to absorb the engine vibrations, but also have to be able to withstand the re-active thrust from the prop.

Most diesel engines have an inherent tendency to vibrate, depending on design and speed. Smoothest are straight six cylinder types and the worst are three cylinder types (even worse than a single cylinder engine). Significantly three cylinder types are smack in the middle of the most useful power range for narrowboats and therefore they are quite a challenge in terms of achieving a suitable flexible mounting.

Very heavy traditional and vintage engines are often too heavy and too badly balanced internally to be put on flexible mounts. Most boat builders therefore, give up on trying to flexibly mount such engines and instead mount them on solid hardwood which takes out a small amount of high frequency vibration.

SILENCING/NOISE INSULATION

One of the main attractions of boating is 'getting away from it all' hence the last thing the steerer needs is the intrusion of engine noise. Narrowboats with a traditional engine room start with an advantage here. Also the sound of a full traditional or vintage diesel is often somewhat pleasing rather than intrusive.

In a conventional layout the so called "hospital silencer" (derived from a design developed for hospital stand-by generators) is very effective at reducing exhaust noise, being a large cylindrical silencer with heavy external acoustic and thermal lagging.

Another significant noise element is the typical diesel engine rattle. Acoustic insulation products can be applied in sheet form to the inside of engine panels and underneath decks to minimise this. These are particularly useful for cruiser and semi-trad boats where the engine is, literally, underfoot.

The Rolls-Royce solution is a fully enclosed acoustic packaged engine set including a 3.5 kVA, 230v generator for mains powering most of the cabin facilities. This also enables a gas-free boat which is sought by some owners.

GEARBOX

Most boats have a contemporary mechanical reduction gearbox to reduce the engine speed to a suitable speed for the propeller. Typically the reduction ratio is between 1.5:1 and 3:1 although examples outside this range can be specified for particular circumstances.

The gearbox is generally bolted directly to the rear engine flywheel housing and the drive taken directly from the rear face of the flywheel. Most have hydraulically engaged clutch drives to make the engagement of forward or reverse a smooth action with a minimal shock load on the drive. It is essential that the gearbox is of adequate size to take the combination of power and torque developed by the engine. Maintenance may require automatic transmission oil top ups for the hydraulic clutch, but some makes use standard engine oil which is more convenient.

DRIVE SHAFT

The output shaft of the gearbox is usually connected to the propeller shaft by a flexible coupling (Centaflex and Pythondrive are well-known examples) and this is a vital part of the transmission system. The coupling performs two main functions; it allows slight misalignment between the gearbox shaft and the propeller shaft, and accommodates forward and back movement by the engine on its flexible mounts, and the thrust of the propeller.

The coupling must be big enough and very resilient to cope with the power, torque and constant flexing in both forwards and reverse directions. In use, failure of the flexible element which is typically a rubber interface, is not uncommon especially after several years of service so it is sensible to keep a spare on board.

The Aquadrive is an alternative coupling system which prevents the thrust of the prop being transferred to the engine, thus making the flexible engine mounts more effective and improving refinement. It transfers prop thrust directly to the hull, and only allows the shortened prop shaft to move in and out of the stern tube.

Boats with a traditional engine room require a long intermediate shaft with a universal joint at each end to transfer the drive to the prop.

PROPELLER

The propeller is self-evidently a vital part of the boat propulsion system, however, selecting a prop is one of the most mysterious areas, with no hard and fast rules due to the several unquantifiable variables involved. Consequently sizing is often referred to as a 'black art'!

On the whole a big boat will need a big prop and vice versa. The bigger the prop the more water it will push past the boat, but it is easy to oversize a prop and then find that the engine runs out of power and torque, or undersize it and find that even with the engine screaming the boat does not have enough speed.

Props are sized by diameter, (overall diameter over the blade tips), and "pitch" – the measure of how much water will be pushed past the prop in one revolution. Typically a narrowboat prop may be specified as 20 x12, i.e. diameter of 20 ins and pitch of 12 ins. The range generally used in narrowboats is 17- 22in diameter and 10–15in pitch.

Painted and polished Lister three cylinder on display in a traditional engine room

Little twin-cylinder Petter was a stalwart diesel power unit on small narrowboats

This water lubricated stern gland is an alternative to the conventional greaser

The popular Barrus Shire is a UK version of the established Yanmar range of marine diesels

Direction of use (the same rotation as the engine for forward travel) and shaft diameter must also be specified. Most inland waterway props are three-bladed turbine types made out of phosphor bronze.

STERN TUBE AND GLAND

The stern tube and gland have the dual purpose of allowing the prop shaft to pass out through the stern and resisting leakage of water back along the shaft. The simplest system consists of inner and outer plain metal bearings in the stern tube which the prop shaft passes through.

At the inside end is a sealing gland packed with graphite treated rope which is compressed onto the propshaft by a sliding packing ring. The bearing surfaces are kept lubricated by grease which also helps seal against water leaking through the gland.

A remote greaser enables the grease to be 'topped up' (normally daily) by a turn or two on the unit, and periodically the packing ring has to be tightened to maintain gland pressure. When all of the adjustment has been used the gland packing must be replaced. This is quite a simple procedure which can usually be undertaken whilst the boat is still afloat.

Some boats have alternative grease-less seals, using a rubber 'cutless' outer bearing which is purely water lubricated and at the inner end of the shaft a second, usually water lubricated sealed bearing.

ALTERNATIVE DRIVE SYSTEMS

Many alternative ideas for boat propulsion have been put forward but there are relatively few that are both practical and affordable:

Hydraulic drive is an established option that allows great flexibility of engine location. There are several designs and methods but in essence the engine drives a hydraulic pump which is connected by hoses or pipes to a hydraulic motor attached directly to the prop shaft.

Thus the engine can be quite a long way from the stern, and in some cases it is mounted in the bows – quieter for the steerer but not for any crew on the front deck!

In the simplest design the engine speed is used to vary speed and a reversing valve achieves reverse. A more controllable but expensive design has the engine running at a constant speed and the prop speed is varied by altering the stroke of the pump. This is more correctly known as a 'hydrostatic' system.

The main advantage is that the prop speed is infinitely variable from very slow rotation to flat out depending on the conditions. Reverse is achieved by reversing the pump cylinders and therefore very slow reverse speed is available.

Even if the engine is mounted a long way from the steerer hydraulic drive is still far from being totally quiet since hydraulic motors and valves also have a characteristic whine, but it is significantly quieter than conventional propulsion systems.

Electric drive has long been thought of as the Holy Grail in boating power, being virtually silent and creating no immediate pollution. So far it has been most successful on smaller boats where there are less electrical demands and in areas where networks of recharging stations have been set up – the Norfolk Broads is at the forefront of providing these.

Usually electric drive consists of a large bank of lead/acid batteries powering a 12-48v DC motor directly connected to the prop shaft with charging via landline, sometimes supplemented by solar panels. Cruising range between charges is necessarily limited.

More developed systems use electric motor and gearbox driven from an extensive battery bank which is charged as before but also by a modern high-speed acoustically sealed generator set. This gives greater range but unfortunately the system's cost is likely to deter many boaters. So far, though, the true go-anywhere, fully equipped electric narrowboat remains elusive.

Electrical systems

Electrics are the adolescents of the boating world. They can be troublesome, awkward and sometimes prone to blowing a fuse. We advise on how best to deal with them

These shorelines in a modern marina provide a reliable AC supply for the moored boats – but be careful, the seemingly simple landline connection can cause serious hull corrosion problems if not connected correctly

The simplest on-board electrical system is a single 12 volt battery used to start the engine and to power a few cabin lights but not a lot more. A stage beyond this sees the provision of separate batteries for starting and domestic needs, plus a shoreline to provide mains AC supply when moored.

However the electrical systems of modern boats have grown like Topsy. A modern live-aboard narrowboat can come complete with everything from microwave oven to washing machine. And, unless you are permanently hooked up to that landline, everything electrical on a boat inevitably leads back to the batteries, whether directly from 12 or 24 volt components or via an inverter that converts battery output to mains AC.

BATTERIES
The first step to understanding boat electrics is to know your batteries. The familiar car type battery is for engine starting or bow thrusters only. It is designed to give a fast release of a lot of energy. However it will deteriorate fast when repeatedly deeply discharged so is unsuitable for powering the domestic features on a boat.

The leisure batteries are of a deep cycle design and have a different internal structure designed to withstand the repeated slow, deep discharges typical of domestic use but won't provide the punch needed for starting. The design does make them more prone to deterioration through sulphation and they need

periodic extended charging to reduce this.

Battery designs are constantly evolving and there is a wide variety of batteries described as traction, semi-traction, leisure or dual-purpose. Wet lead acid batteries are the traditional batteries we all know. Some have removable cell caps so you can top them up but many are now permanently sealed.

Absorbed Glass Mat (AGM) batteries are still wet lead acid, but the acid is held in glass fibre wadding. They are supposed to suffer less from higher

charge and discharge rates and less sulphation.

Gel batteries have their acid in jelly form and are popular with long distance sailors, however the cost is likely to rule these out for the average inland boater. They also need a different charging regime to other types for maximum life and effect.

Both AGM and Gel batteries charge quickly and are less prone to self-discharge or suphation if left uncharged. On the other hand they are more expensive and potentially have shorter lives. Don't mix battery types in the same bank and remember that with batteries, as with most things in life, you get what you pay for.

Unfortunately a battery – even a deep-cycle one – should not be expected to actually supply its rated amp hours of electricity. The more often and the deeper you discharge typical domestic batteries below 50 per cent, the more you shorten their life.

In addition how fully an alternator will charge the battery depends upon the age of its design, with newer ones performing better. The rate of charge of a battery also tails off as it becomes more fully charged and require advanced alternator controllers to maximise.

A sensible, conservative view is to assume that your system will only charge your battery to about 80 per cent of maximum. So, all in all, you can only expect to use 30 per cent of the battery's rated capacity (the 80 per cent maximum down to 50 per cent charge level). So, aside from waiting until your batteries are flat, how do you know if your electrical system is adequate?

ENERGY AUDIT
The answer is the energy audit, a piece of electrical accountancy that will let us know how much you are taking out of the batteries and how much you are putting back. All boaters should do one on their boats and review it when they add electrical equipment or they will have no real idea about electrical loads.

The audit generally covers the 'leisure' or domestic equipment batteries. You can ignore the engine electrics as long as you have separate alternators or a split charging system.

The audit is a list of the boat's electrical equipment with a record of how much current each draws in a typical day.

Motors are likely to have their amperage on the label, but most items will be labelled in Watts, which can be converted by the formula **AMPS = WATTS /VOLTS**. Divide the wattage by 12 or 24 depending upon the voltage of your system for all non-inverter driven loads. For inverter driven loads divide by 10 or 20, to allow for the inefficiency within the inverter.

THE POWER AUDIT

Equipment	Amps	Hours*	Amp hours
Lights (3 x 1.8 amps)	5.4	5	27
TV	3	4	12
Water pump	5	1	5
Fridge (12v)**	2.8	12	34
Radio	1	3	3
TOTAL	81 ah		

* Use spring or autumn days for your calculations when cruising hours are shorter and lights used more.

** A fridge has a thermostat so we can assume that it is actually running for only about half the day.

A modern, well-planned electrical cupboard with 12 DC fuse panel, mains AC consumer unit and control unit for the AC engine alternator

ELECTRICITY BASICS

AMPS
The Amp is the unit of electric current. It is a physical count of how many electrons are flowing down a cable. Amps are never destroyed or lost. If 5 amps left the battery and flowed through the circuit, 5 amps would have to return to the battery.

VOLTS
Voltage provides the "push" to force the electrons to flow around the wires. It's this push that gets used up when electricity does work, so whenever work is done the voltage gets used up or drops. Sometimes too much of that push gets used up simply pushing electrons around the cables of the boat and 'volt drop' becomes a problem.

DC AND AC
Current from batteries and alternators always flows in one direction, from positive to negative by convention. In AC (alternating current) the current flow constantly reverses direction. This enables high voltages to be sent longer distances and is the basis of domestic electric supply.

WATTS
Most people know it as the measurement of how bright a bulb will be or how hot an electric fire will get. It is the unit of power or work.

Volts, amps and watts are linked by the formula:

Watts = Volts x Amps or
Watts divided by Volts = Amps.

If something reduces the voltage (typically volt drop) less current will flow so less electrical power is available to the appliance and it will not work as well as it should or may refuse to work at all.

OHMS
Ohms are the measure of resistance which, as its name implies, is what restricts current flow. A high resistance such as a low wattage bulb will only allow a small current flow.

AMP HOUR
This indicates how much electricity a battery will hold. A 110ah (amp hour) battery is theoretically capable of supplying 110 amps for one hour. Note the word 'theoretically'.

Remember that the calculated 81ah will be only 30 per cent of the rated capacity so the boat will need 270 ah worth of batteries – supplied by 3 x 110ah for example.

The next thing to consider is if this amount of electricity that can be put back into the batteries during the period you are prepared to run your engine – let's say three hours a day.

Batteries require anything between ten and 40 per cent more electricity put back in than was taken out as energy conversion is never 100 per cent efficient so to put 81ah back into the battery the charging system needs to supply about 106 amp hours. To do that in three hours running time requires an average input of (106/3) or 36amps. This implies an alternator with a quoted output of around 70 amps.

The faster you try to charge a battery above a certain rate the more you will shorten its life. Somewhere around 25 per cent of rated capacity is a consensus maximum.

The 330 amp hours worth of domestic battery bank could be charged at a little under 100 amps without damaging the batteries, so everything balances. If it had not, the energy audit would provide the information to consider options like fitting another battery.

WIRING
Good wiring is at the heart of reliable, safe and efficient on-board electrics. First step is to size wiring correctly. Don't be misled by the quoted current rating of a cable – it is simply the current it can carry without catching fire. It says nothing about how much voltage would be lost trying to push the current through long cables – voltage drop.

Voltage drop can be a problem on narrowboats with their long cable runs or when cables are too thin, so electricity has to work hard just to get through the wire.

It can be hard to trace, especially on equipment that requires a high starting current (like a modern fridge which draw hundreds of amps for a split second as it starts up and then settles down to a fairly low current draw.) Batteries and charging systems often get blamed for inadequate wiring.

For example, that fridge will need to be wired in supply and return cable with a conductor cross sectional area of 1mm sq. for each metre between the battery and fridge which means you will probably require some hefty cabling.

Things like lamps and other low current circuits will normally be fine with 2mm² cable, but any motor, heater or other item that causes large current

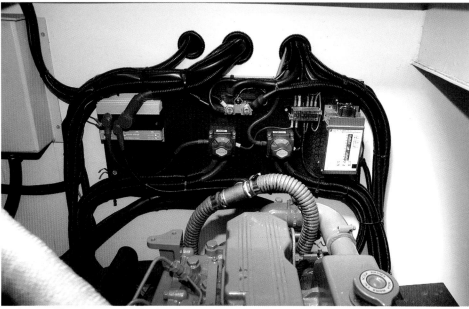

Easily accessible isolator switches for the engine and domestic batteries are a mandatory safety requirement – these are installed on the forward bulkhead of the engine compartment

flows will need properly calculated cable size using this formula:

**Voltdrop = 0.0164 x cable length (metres)
x amps conductor area (sq mm)**

Voltage drop should be between 0.3 and 0.5v maximum.

FUSES

Every circuit should have a fuse or circuit breaker fitted that is rated to protect the cable – NOT the appliance. This should be as near to the battery as reasonably possible to minimise the length of unprotected cable. Neat wiring, properly clipped in place with either soldered or correctly crimped connectors (use a quality crimping tool) will minimise the chance of electrical problems – and impress a future buyer.

AC ELECTRICITY

More and more people want 220v AC (mains) power on board their boat. Unfortunately once you get mains on the boat the pressure to add more and more "domestic" items becomes difficult to resist, and that careful power audit goes out of the window!

Mains electricity when away from the umbilical shoreline is provided either from the batteries via a DC to AC inverter or directly from the engine using an engine-driven AC generator or a combination of both. Another (even more costly) option is the stand-alone generator set linked (often by a programmed system) to the other electrical systems.

The inverter does not produce AC electricity, it converts the batteries' DC supply to AC so AC usage will drain batteries unless they are recharged (something which boaters can forget). The AC generator has a strong output and does not drain batteries, allowing power-hungry devices to be used – though only when cruising.

WHAT SORT OF INVERTER?

Any inverter needs to use some current to make itself work over and above the current it is converting. It will use this amount of current if it is being used to produce 3000 watts or less than half an amp. An inverter that is quoted as 90 per cent efficient probably is just that at close to

maximum output, but at low outputs it is likely to be much less so. In operation it will also generate heat so correct installation is crucial.

The simplest and cheapest inverters are of the modified sine wave type. They will be fine running 'basic' AC items like heaters and phone chargers or single speed power tools but items using electronics may not work so the more costly pure sine wave type will be a better investment.

Commonly the inverter and battery charger can be found combined in a 'combi' unit but this has the disadvantage of leaving you in a sticky situation should the unit fail. Likewise if you are planning a liveaboard with large electricity requirements, two medium size inverters rather than one large unit provides you with an emergency 'fall-back' supply should one fail.

SHORELINE POWER

This seemingly simple source of mains power needs careful installation. It is vital that if you have more than one source of AC power it should be impossible to have them turned on together, as mixing shore lines, inverters and generators brings complications.

Typically a purpose designed high current loading double pole two or three way switch is used, but there are automatic systems and other methods.

When a shoreline is wired in to a permanent 230v on-board system you also connect the earthing of your boat's hull to every other nearby boat's hull that uses a shoreline and galvanic corrosion can occur. Your anodes may start to protect all the other boats in the marina or if you do not have adequate anodes fitted and the steel alloy of your boat is a little different to some others, your hull gets eaten away. For boats that spend long periods attached to shorelines it can be a significant issue.

The Rolls Royce solution is to use an isolation transformer at the mains entry point, but as these are expensive many people rely upon galvanic isolators placed in the shoreline earth cable at the entry point to your boat. Always use one that has a built-in means of checking operation so that you know it is working.

This completely self-sufficient liveaboard has no less than six batteries for starting and leisure use, charged by twin engine alternators and a stand-alone generator unit

PROTECTION AND EARTHING

To protect from shocks caused by faulty insulation, damp etc a Residual Current Device (RCD) is fitted as close to the source of AC power as possible.

In the event of a circuit or appliance failure the RCD will almost instantly detect it has happened and trip out before you can get a shock. To do this the current must have another way to flow back to the inverter\shoreline\generator and this is the purpose of the earth wire. If there is no earth (or a faulty one) the RCD will be useless.

On a steel boat the inverter earth is connected to the metal structure of the boat at the same point as the 12/24v negative connection. The shoreline input should be similarly earthed to the hull – it will already be earthed to the hull if an inverter or generator is also fitted. This will then ensure it is not possible to electrocute anyone when they step on or off a boat with a mains fault.

All metal fittings such as taps and gas pipes are also "bonded" to earth, as is done at home.

From the RCD onwards fuses or circuit breakers protect each circuit but remember they are there to protect the cable, so make sure they are not rated at more that the cable's current rating. Run all mains cables inside trunking and label it as mains.

BATTERY CHARGING

Many new narrowboat engines come ready fitted with twin alternators; one to charge the engine battery and a larger output unit to charge the domestic batteries. However the boat with a single alternator and domestic as well as engine batteries needs to apportion the charge and make sure that one battery set doesn't discharge into the other.

Traditionally this has been done by the split-charge diode. A diode only allows electricity to pass one way through it, so two can be wired to enable the alternator to charge the batteries, but prevent one battery bank discharging itself through the other.

As soon as alternator output voltage becomes higher than the battery voltage, the relevant diode will open and allow charge to that bank. When the alternator output voltage is higher than either battery voltage, both batteries will be receiving their correct proportion of the charge.

Unfortunately the system is not terribly

Above: tidy control panel for small Sea Otter

Above: how not to do it – scattered, untidy wiring

Above: And more of the same

efficient. Most modern alternators measure their output voltage inside themselves, so any resistance between alternator and battery will lower the charging voltage and thus decrease charging current. If you are using a split charge diode you will lose something like half a volt across the diode. As the years go on you will also lose voltage across the master switch and probably across loose/dirty connections.

An advanced controller is vital if you are using split charge diodes. It should convert your alternator to battery sensing and then the output voltage rises to overcome any resistance in the circuit to "fully charge" your batteries.

An advanced controller should also get the batteries more fully charged and thus slow down the rate of deterioration through sulphation. Advanced controllers should also bring the battery to maximum charge faster than an alternator's inbuilt voltage regulator alone. An advanced controller of competent design is a definite advantage and would tend to make the system more fault tolerant.

However one that simply holds the charge at a high level for a prolonged period of time can cause overheated batteries and constant topping up. The controller should pulse alternator output up by half a volt or so for about 15 minutes and then given the same period of rest at the "normal" charging voltage.

The system should also carry out monitoring battery temperature and state of charge to ensure no damage occurs.

There are arguments that the modern alternator's inbuilt regulator reduces the need for an advanced controller and that there are better charge-management alternatives to split-charge diodes. Take advice from more than one source before choosing one.

LANDLINE CHARGING

If the boater has very large battery banks, is a live-aboard, or wants minimum involvement with the system, then a two or three stage marine charger is probably their best option.

If the boater has a modest battery bank, just wants the batteries fully charged for the next weekend, is happy to keep a bit of an eye on the charger, then an automotive unit with polarised plug fitted to the boat's wiring should be fine. A modern two or three stage charger can be left on indefinitely and will tell you when it thinks the batteries are fully charged by LED or warning lamp.

The main thing to watch is that the charger has sufficient output to do more than float charge the batteries. A 4 amp charger on a five bank battery will probably not actually charge the batteries; simply prevent them self discharging: 8 to 10 amps is a minimum for proper charging.

POINTS TO REMEMBER

Always remember that 'mains' AC electricity can kill and that mains electric and water are a particularly lethal mixture. Follow these key rules:
● Never work on mains circuits unless you are certain you know what you are doing.
● Never work on mains circuits if you are alone on the boat – make sure you have someone close by who knows what to do in the event of an accident.
● Get help from a qualified electrician – not the local 'expert' – if you are at all unsure.

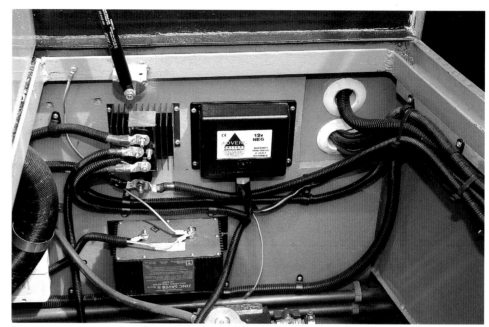

Battery management unit, top right of picture, optimises battery charging. Galvanic isolator unit, bottom centre, prevents corrosion caused by shoreline connections

Built-in generator, bottom of picture, is used to supply heavy AC loads such as washing machine

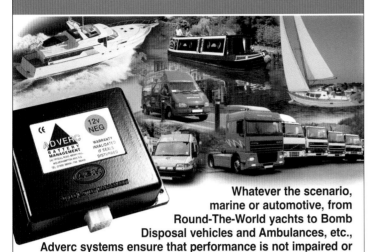

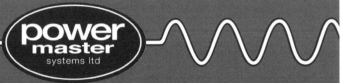
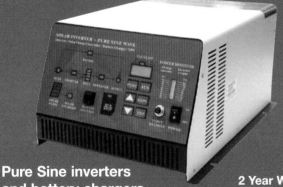

Plumbing & heating

Hot water and heating systems have become as sophisticated on modern boats as they are in houses. We take a look at everything – including the kitchen sink

The wood burning stove is a fine source of heat. Oil versions are cleaner in use but more costly to run

Calorifiers in all their various shapes and sizes are the heart of every narrowboat's hot water system

Boats on the inland waterways have become increasingly sophisticated and complex. Many owners now install much of the domestic equipment they have in their own homes. Some boats now come complete with full size cookers, central heating and even washing machines. In this section we take a look at the services that supply this equipment: hot and cold water, heating and the provision of a gas supply.

WATER SUPPLY
Canal boats have a holding tank for their fresh water, usually mounted in the bows below the well deck. Some are an integral part of the hull and require periodic maintenance, cleaning and re-blacking which is a messy job. Others are made from stainless steel or plastic and virtually maintenance free, though additional sterilising of the water is sensible if

the system is not in regular use. A filler point for the tank is mounted in the well deck area or on the adjacent gunwale.

The tank can be filled with water from standpipes which are widely distributed around the canal system and at marinas etc. Most tanks hold around 100/150 gallons of water which can last a couple of days or longer, depending on usage.

An electric water pump feeds water from the tank to the sink, basin, shower, bath etc. The pump operates automatically as taps are turned on and off. The pump is often located near to the water tank or under a kitchen unit in the galley. It is powered by the boat's 12 volt electrical system. An accumulator is generally fitted to regulate flow and pressure.

Plumbing pipework is almost entirely in plastic these days: it is easy to install and less prone to freezing (but must always be cut with the correct

cutting tool). Well designed pipework is always made as accessible as possible so it can be repaired or altered without dismantling half the interior of the boat!

WATER HEATING
Most boats have provision for heating water. The two most common ways of providing hot water on canal boats are by means of an instantaneous gas water heater or by a calorifier. Instantaneous gas fired water heaters – Paloma is one of the best known – were very popular in the past and are still widely used as they are very effective.

The heater is usually located in the galley and piped into the boat water and gas systems. When the hot water tap is opened the heater fires up automatically and piping hot water flows from the tap. They can be used to provide hot water for showers, baths and basins as well as the kitchen sink.

However 'open-flued' water heaters of this type are no longer acceptable under the safety regulations for new boats. Existing units can be serviced on a boat but new ones cannot be fitted.

Heating the water by a calorifier has become increasingly popular. A calorifier is a small tank, typically 12 to 14 gallons capacity, similar to the hot water cylinder in your home.

Water in the calorifier is heated by passing engine cooling water through a coil within the tank – again like your home boiler heats domestic water. As the engine heats up, water from the cooling system passes through the coil and transfers heat to the domestic water. Effectively it is 'free heat' as this would otherwise be wasted by the engine cooling system. A secondary coil can be linked to the boat's heating boiler or stove.

Calorifiers can be vertical or horizontal and are usually mounted either in the engine room, in a cupboard or even under a bed. The downside is that the engine (or heating boiler) has to be run to heat the water. This can be inconvenient both for yourself and others if the engine needs to be run while moored up, and simply idling the engine to warm the water is also not good for its long-term health. As a result

Plumbing pipes and valves should be accessible; this complex system is in a purpose-designed cupboard

The macerator pump-out toilet seen here 'does exactly what it says on the tin'. Need we say more? It is a sophisticated but costly option that will reduce emptying frequency of holding tank

calorifiers can be fitted with 220v mains AC immersion heaters, though this in turn demands a source of high output AC on the boat.

Other types of water heaters can be found on canal craft such as stored gas water heaters. Here gas is used to heat a small amount of water stored in a tank and connected to the domestic water system. However, their use is not very common and most boats are equipped with either an instantaneous gas water heater or a calorifier.

Hot water plumbing must be done with care – the calorifier must be fitted with a pressure relief valve and the whole water system needs drain points so it can be 'winterised' if the boat is left unused.

SHOWERS

In the past small 'hip' baths were generally fitted to narrowboats but showers are now almost universal as they take up less space and standard domestic fittings can often be used. A thermostatic mixing valve is almost essential to prevent temperature fluctuations if other taps are used.

Whether bath or shower a pump is needed to take away the waste water. There are different types: the old style sump type being generally replaced by an in-line impeller type which is less prone to blockage but must not be allowed to run when dry (so is usually operated by a bell-push type button.)

TOILETS

There are a number of options when it comes to choosing toilet facilities on boats but broadly they divide into cassette and pump-out. The least costly and most easily installed is the cassette type toilet. This is a mounted in unit with its own small waste collection tank. The tank is charged with a measured amount of chemical which breaks down the waste matter and reduces any odours. In the most basic types, the top section of the toilet contains its own, refillable supply of flushing water.

Due to the small size of the tank it needs frequent emptying and recharging with chemical. However it can be emptied (usually) free of charge at facilities provided around the system by BW and marinas. It also requires no installation other than placing in a convenient position in the bathroom. Even if a more sophisticated toilet if fitted, it can be a useful back-up or secondary toilet.

A more developed version of the cassette toilet has become increasingly popular. It is more like a traditional toilet both in use and looks, and is permanently installed in the bathroom and plumbed into the water supply for flushing.

The cassette tank is larger and requires less frequent emptying. Alternatively, a vacuum cassette system uses a vacuum pump to draw waste to a remote cassette. Spare tanks can be purchased so there is not a problem if you are unable to get to an emptying point.

The second basic type is the pump out toilet. In the simplest arrangement (the 'dump through' type) a ceramic toilet bowl is mounted directly on top of a fixed holding tank which is built into the boat. Tanks are available in mild steel, stainless steel and plastic.

The toilet is plumbed into the water supply for flushing and the waste is flushed through into the holding tank. This is charged with chemicals to break down the waste and reduce odours however a downside is that odours can come through from the tank into the bathroom when the toilet is flushed.

Oil fired Aga style cast-iron stove also heats water and directly warms boat

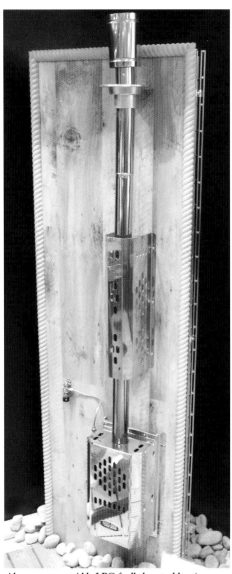

Above: compact Alde LPG-fuelled central heating boiler is a popular alternative to oil heating

Below: the Envirolet composting is an eco-friendly alternative. It is odour free, needs minimal attention and generates dry compost. Snags are size and price

A more refined version uses a remote holding tank to which the waste matter is drawn by vacuum from the toilet. With this type of installation there is very little odour and its use is very similar to a domestic toilet. It is more expensive to install than the pump out toilet discussed previously, though the boatbuilder has much more flexibility in design and location and it also requires periodic emptying.

The tank can be quite large and therefore requires less frequent emptying than cassette toilets However, emptying it requires a visit to a boatyard or marina that has pump out facilities and there is generally a charge for this service.

BW has also provided a number of self pump out installations around the canal system where owners can pump out the holding tank themselves at a much reduced cost. Some areas of the canal system do, though, have fewer pump-out facilities than others so 'convenience' is a factor in choice of individual systems.

Finally, a further development is the composting toilet, which has been installed on a number of canal boats. This breaks the waste matter down into a dry, compost like material that can be removed and used on the garden etc. It is environmentally friendly, requires little intervention by the boat owner and does not require chemicals in use. Unfortunately they are a little on the large side for most boats and not the most aesthetically attractive. They also consume electrical power to drive a ventilation fan which may present a problem on some boats.

HEATING

Given the vagaries of the weather in this country there can be few boats that don't have some kind of space heating installed. Perhaps the most popular, over recent years, has been the installation of a solid fuel or multi fuel stove. These are relatively cheap to purchase and install and can easily provide sufficient warmth for a canal boat. They can burn a variety of fuels including wood, peat and coal, although most manufactures recommend smokeless fuel for best results.

These stoves are often fitted with a back boiler that can be connected to two or three radiators which spread the heat more evenly around the boat. With practice and experience

they can be fuelled so as to remain alight over night. They are quite efficient and economical to run and make an attractive focal point. However, the heat output fluctuates widely and they produce a lot of dust and ash. They need frequent refuelling and require a ready supply of wood or coal etc.

Their greatest advantage is simplicity. So long as you have matches and can glean some wood from the canalside, you won't be cold. Central heating systems on boats can (and do) fail!

Stoves similar to multi-fuel stoves are available that use diesel as the fuel. These diesel fired stoves also look attractive and provide a focal point in the saloon. Indeed some have replica coals or are converted from the multi-fuel stoves mentioned above.

The fuel feed is taken either from a diesel tank specially installed for the purpose or the tank supplying the engine. (A separate tank might be useful if the tax-free 'red diesel' boat fuel dispensation ends, as it might.)

The heat output is controllable enabling the boat to be easily maintained at the desired temperature. They need little maintenance and are clean to operate. They can be fitted with a back boiler and connected to radiators and also to a coil on the calorifier for hot water. They are more expensive to purchase and install than a multi-fuel stove but have gained in popularity because they need so little maintenance and cleaning and are relatively easy to light.

Miniature diesel-fired boilers (Eberspacher, Mikuni etc) are also popular. These are usually installed in the engine room with a diesel feed from the main fuel tank. They heat water which is pumped through a series of radiators positioned along the boat and they can also be connected to a calorifier to heat water for domestic use. Some can work rather like a car heater, warming air rather than water which is blown via ducts to areas of the boat but these are more commonly found on smaller craft.

It is also possible to use liquid petroleum gas (LPG) to fuel a hot water boiler which can be fitted into a cupboard or other confined space. Alde is the best known.

All types are easy and clean to use and require no daily maintenance. Their small size makes them unobtrusive and easy to accommodate. They

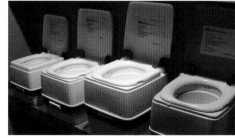

Simplest of toilets: the Porta Potti in various sizes

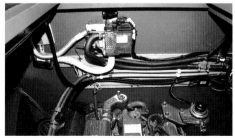

Central heating unit installed in engine compartment

Shower has overtaken bath in popularity; it saves space in bathroom and often domestic units can be fitted

are, though, considerably more expensive to purchase than a multi-fuel stove and they also consume electrical power when operating to drive pumps and fans. Gas driven boilers will require pretty regular changes of cylinder, too.

It is possible to find boats with other forms of heating such as gas fires and catalytic heaters but these are becoming increasingly rare as multi fuel stoves and diesel-fired heating have gained in popularity.

GAS SYSTEM

There are very few canal boats that are not equipped with an LPG supply provided by either butane or propane gas cylinders. Propane being the most popular as it continues to work in cold temperatures unlike butane. The gas bottles are stored in a purpose-built locker, frequently at the bow, but in some designs on the rear deck or in the case of cruiser-style boats mounted on the transom.

The location and construction of lockers for storing gas bottles, is closely specified by current regulations including the Boat Safety Scheme. LPG is heavier than air and any leakage has the potential to build up in the bilges of a boat where it presents a safety hazard. For this reason a large section of the Boat Safety Scheme is focused on the installation of the gas system and its equipment, thereby helping reduce the risks to the absolute minimum. Work on gas systems should also only be undertaken by CORGI qualified personnel.

LPG is most frequently used on boats for cooking and to a lesser extent heating. It is difficult to find a more cost effective and reliable

A fully fitted utility room like this one is useful on a liveaboard boat but poses complicated extra plumbing and electrical issues. A second toilet, as here, should offer an alternative disposal method to the main toilet

alternative to LPG when it comes to cooking. Many boats have domestic size hobs and ovens installed and LPG is a very convenient fuel for this purpose. Provided the regulations regarding installation and use are followed, the risks to boaters are very small.

A number of boat owners have attempted to eliminate gas from their boats by installing alternative equipment such as diesel-fired cookers and heating. While diesel heating has proved increasingly popular and very effective, diesel cookers have been much less popular.

They are more expensive to purchase and do not supply the instant heat of a gas cooker.

Cooking with electricity has also been tried on a small number of boats. This requires the installation of a large engine driven generator to provide power for the cooker, meaning the boat engine has to be run when power is required for cooking, or a separate, diesel generator unit which has to be run.

Again this is a considerably more expensive option than a gas cooker and not without risks of its own. Hence most owners have taken the decision that gas cooking treated with care and respect is the best option.

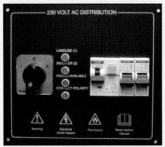

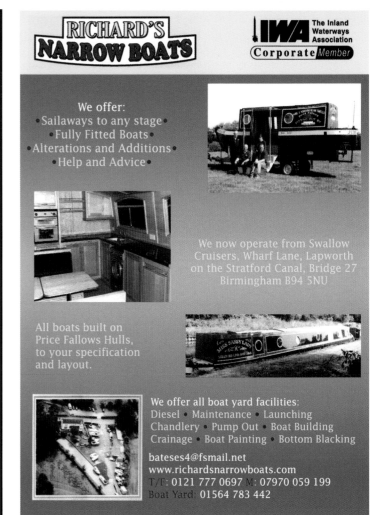

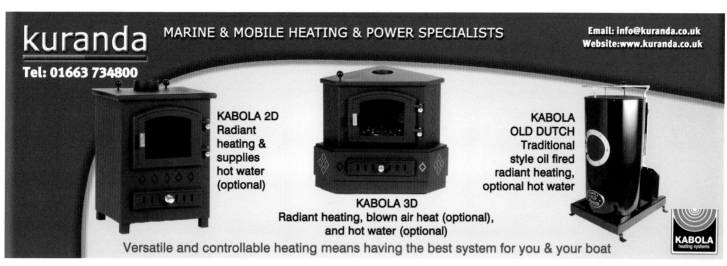

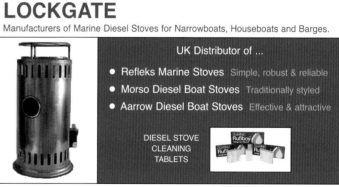

Accessories and options

We advise on the upgrades, extras and essential accessories that are all part of the finished narrowboat

This 50hp Isuzu engine is a powerful upgrade but would be worthwhile for river use

Spot the bow thrusters in action! The tell-tale side-wake always gives it away

A cratch and cover can create a delightful seating area in the bows

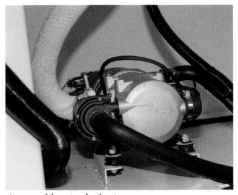

A central heating boiler is very useful for all year round boaters

BOW THRUSTERS

At £2500+, bow thrusters are a costly option and one that tends to bring out the worst in other boaters. The sound of a thruster being used to nudge a boat into a lock does very often say something about the competency of the steerer. If you can handle a boat well, you probably don't need one on a narrowboat (but might on a wide beam boat). On the other hand, if you feel nervous, have a full length boat or simply want the reassurance, then why not?

Electric thrusters are too easy to over-use, leading to overheated cables. The more expensive hydraulic type can be used continuously should you want to perform pirouettes on the water. If you are not sure whether you really need thrusters, ask for a tube to be installed in your new boat for about £600, then you can always change your mind if you find you can't operate the craft without one.

CRATCH AND COVERS

A fully enclosed front deck effectively turn the bow cockpit into an extension of the cabin which is useful, especially in poor weather – though a glazed cratch board and clear panels in the vinyl sides can be a pleasant place to sit at any time. It's a £700+ option but probably one of the most valuable to have – since it is much appreciated by buyers when it comes to sell on.

CRUISING GEAR

A whole variety of essential accessories come under this heading. Let's start with fenders: every boat will need front and rear fenders and in narrowboats they are traditionally plaited and knotted from rope. The front is often a 'sausage' shape and at the rear, large 'pudding' fenders protrude out to protect the rudder. Both are attached with a weak link in their mounting chains in case of snagging.

Strictly narrowboats don't need side fenders as the rubbing strakes on the hull sides offer protection and fenders can also foul on tight lock walls. However, slim rubber tube fenders will protect against chafing during mooring and yet still allow access through most locks if they are left hanging.

A boarding plank, pole and boathook are all essential kit and stored on the boat's roof. They should be located positively in place rather than allowed to slide around. The pole should be used for pushing the boat off when grounded or punting it along but not for fending off another boat. You can't divert a 15 ton narrowboat with a length of wood!

Finally, mooring lines: traditional ropes were in natural materials like hemp and sisal but now man-made fibres rule. You get what you pay for: cheap poly-propylene ropes are rough to use and crude looking while the best man-made ropes replicate almost perfectly the traditional look if that's what you want.

For cruising, you need front and rear lines, probably around 25-35 feet long, as well as a centre line if your boat is equipped with a suitable roof mounting. A spare long line is useful for deep locks. Have a pair of correct length permanent mooring lines made up with spliced ends to fit your boat to leave at your permanent base. They will save your cruising lines from wear and tear and can be made from durable cheap rope.

ENGINES AND GEARBOXES

Most narrowboats around 55ft have about a 35hp engine as standard. A bigger engine can be useful on rivers like the tidal Thames or Trent where a smaller one may not have the grunt needed to push against an ebbing tide. The bigger engine will also sound very relaxed at canal speed. It might also be better able to cope with ancillary devices, such as additional 230V alternator and hydraulic take-offs for bow thrusters.

However, the smaller engine will be more fuel efficient. On some canals, a large engine may only be running just above tickover, which might lead to long-term damage from oil sludging.

An upgraded instrument panel – ideally with oil pressure, voltmeter and temperature gauges as a minimum, backed-up by warning lights and buzzers, is a must.

MAINS POWER

Providing substantial mains AC power for a boat is expensive so judging what is required is essential. Most new boats have the ability to 'hook-up' to shore-side 230v supplies – through a proper RCCB system for protection and a galvanic isolator to prevent hull corrosion. Beyond this a small inverter of around 1000w will often suffice to convert battery DC to 220v AC and power a vacuum cleaner, washer or TV. A sine wave type is essential for anything that has electronics (including programming

The rear pudding fender is usually
made of rope and protects the rudder

All boats using rivers are required
to have an anchor readily available for use

Remove dog before throwing into water!

Electrics upgrades are well worth considering for
well used boats

Good quality and well looked after
mooring lines are safe and good to use

A pole is an essential piece of kit
and should always be properly stowed

switches in things like washing machines.)

Some form of battery charger is usually built-in –
a smart 4 stage charger is a good idea – anything from
10A upwards. A 'combi' unit combines inverter and
charger. A larger battery bank is needed and usually a
sophisticated alternator charge controller. More
expensive options include an engine driven AC
generator or even a separate diesel-generator
(expensive at around £8000+ a time!). See Section
14 'Electrics' for full details on choosing electrical
equipment.

HEATING
Many boats have just one source of heating, if any. If
you are away for just the summer months, a single
solid fuel stove in the saloon, with hot water from an
engine heated calorifier, might be all that you need.
For real depth of winter heat, radiator central heating
is a must. Gas fired is quick, clean and uses very little
electricity, but is expensive to run. Diesel fired can be
drip fed – tricky to get started, but can run
unattended for days, though the heaters are quite
bulky. Forced air (Eberspächer, Webasto and Mikuni),
can be very hard on the batteries and some are noisy.

PAINTWORK
The most important part of the paintwork is often
given the least attention: the hull paint. The hull
takes most of the bashing and needs the most
protection. Having the shell grit-blasted, proper two-
part epoxy paint and decent sized magnesium anodes
from the start will increase the lifespan of the vessel
before major surgery is needed. It will probably need

less docking and painting in the future. Expensive, at
over £1000, but the costs saved over the years will
add up, and it is very impressive for potential future
owners. Worth having done, if your builder offers it.

RECESSED PANELS
Recessed cabin side panels simulate the structure of a
wooden topped narrowboat, with its substantial
framing and infill panels. Along with 'rivets' they are
an essential part of a modern-day replica but being
expensive – around £150 a foot for the two sides –
their use tends to be restricted to the rear side panels
carrying the boat's name on other craft.

SAFETY GEAR
Normal safety equipment for an inland boat will
comprise a life ring usually stowed on the roof near
the steerer. On a canal it would probably not be tied
by rope to the roof as the boat will need time to
manoeuvre and return to the person who has fallen
in. On a fast-flowing river it is sensible to have the
life ring attached.

An anchor, ready for use, is a requirement for
river travel and normally attached by chain and
rope. The Danforth type works well and stows flat.
A mud weight can be a useful substitute when
conditions allow.

Life jackets are optional on canals but should be
used for all children. All crew should use them on
tidal rivers or in similarly hazardous conditions.

SECURITY
It is surprising how many people leave their very

expensive boat full of expensive and portable effects
like flat-screen TV sets and cameras protected only
by a small padlock or flimsy bolts. It is not difficult to
have front and rear doors built with proper security
locks and, of course, valuables should always be
kept out of sight – a 'secret' security box is always a
good idea.

In addition, a new generation of alarm systems
has arrived on the market which need minimal
battery power and can notify the owner by SMS text
message if an intruder is on their boat using door
and/or movement sensors to detect their presence.

SOUND INSULATION
The throbbing sound of a diesel engine can become
intrusive on a journey, especially if the boat has a
semi-trad or cruiser stern with the engine underfoot.
Hence useful additions to the spec are a hospital
silencer and proper marine sound insulation of the
engine compartment.

TELEVISION
If you enjoy your Eastenders, the cut can be a
frustrating place as you search for the best reception.
Television aerials range from the crude – a house
aerial on a pole which a crew member turns until you
shout 'stop!' to fully motorised satellite finders costing
around £2000. A neat in-between option is provided
by Maxview which offers a compact roof aerial that
can be adjusted for position and angle from inside the
boat via a handle and gearing system, costing around
£300-£400 (though a system like this has to be
designed into the boat.)

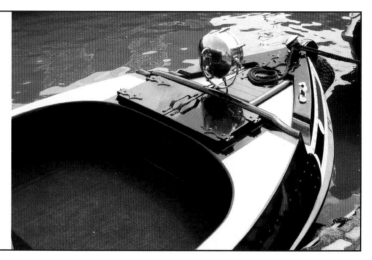

AJ CANOPIES

Established 1978

Braunston

Boat Cover Manufacturers

"Superior Quality Workmanship"

We specialise in all types of boat covers & accessories

'Our business covers your pleasure'

Cross Lane, Braunston, Nr. Daventry, Northants. NN11 7HH

www.ajcanopies.com

01788 890651

Running your boat

Many people buy a narrowboat without ever having laid a hand on a tiller so here we offer some basic guidance

The Gloucester & Sharpness Canal, seen here at Gloucester Docks is wide enough for coastal shipping

Narrowboating is possible through the centre of many cities, including London here on the Regents Canal

In this increasingly regulated world, it is possible simply to buy a boat, whether it is a massive Dutch barge or a tiny Freeman cruiser and drive it without the need for lessons or passing a test. Even those who have been side-swiped by an errant narrowboater would, on balance, probably prefer to keep it that way.

All the same, it is probably a good idea to understand some of the fundamentals before wobbling off along the cut!

LICENCE AND INSURANCE
You might not need to pass a test but you will need a licence – a navigation licence from the authority which runs the waterways on which you want to cruise. This will generally be British Waterways which runs the canal system, and many connecting rivers including the Severn, Trent and Yorkshire Ouse, or the Environment Agency which is in charge of the Thames and East Anglian rivers. You can buy a Gold Licence which covers both.

The Broads are controlled by their own Authority, as are some smaller waterways and you will need visitor licences if you use these. The cost of a licence depends on the size of the boat and how it is powered, as well as where you want to cruise.

As detailed in Section 3, you will need a Boat Safety Scheme certificate and where appropriate an RCD declaration of conformity as well as third-party insurance.

MOORINGS

Moorings are often overlooked by would-be boat owners. Unless you are cruising continuously around the waterways (and that does not mean going back and forth along the same stretch), you will need somewhere to keep your boat when not in use. This can be in a marina or at a designated long-term canal towpath or riverside mooring. In other places along canals and rivers mooring periods are limited – and policed with increasing efficiency.

Moorings are in high demand in some popular areas and waiting lists are common. It is strongly recommended that you have a mooring sorted out before you buy a boat. Most moorings are not transferable, so you will not inherit a mooring even if you buy a secondhand boat – if the seller says otherwise check with BW.

If you plan to live permanently on your boat you need to have a mooring which permits this: many do not and you may have to leave your boat for one or more nights a week.

Mooring prices vary widely, depending on location and the facilities on offer. You can find a comprehensive list of marinas and moorings at British Waterways website www.waterscape.com

CRUISING BASICS

River cruisers and Dutch barges usually have wheel steering but though this may seem reassuringly familiar to car drivers, boats react more slowly than a car travelling at an equivalent speed, so thinking ahead is essential. Also unlike a car, a boat will pivot around its centre, which may be disconcerting if you are steering from the front of a Broads holiday boat and is even odd if your steering position is amidships – you will probably find your stern clipping the nearside bank from time to time until you are used to it.

Narrowboats are, of course, steered with a tiller that is directly connected to the boat's rudder. Moving the tiller left will steer the boat to the right, and vice versa. This is always confusing at first to beginners but it soon becomes second nature. Again the boat pivots around its centre point so bear that in mind when positioning. Forward planning is even more important on a long narrowboat, especially near tight bridges and narrow locks.

The 'rule of the road' is to keep to the right when passing other boats. At other times it is generally easiest to stay in the deepest part of the water – usually the centre, or the outside of bends. This is less important on wide, deep rivers, but can be critical on some canals where depth can be limited in places.

Maximum speed on canals and many rivers is four mph, though higher speed limits will be posted on larger or tidal rivers. Though the speed limit may be low, the golden rule is to slow down when passing moored boats. It's commonsense really, even a shallow wave can spill a hot cup of coffee off of a table. And the canals are not a place for anyone in a hurry!

MANOEUVRING

This is where the novice – and sometimes even the experienced boater – can have problems from time to time. If you are in difficulties with a planned manoeuvre, don't panic, just straighten the boat up and have a quiet re-think. Try to be confident – a boat always steers more accurately when under way; if it's hardly moving it will be at the mercy of any wind or current.

Boats don't come with brakes, of course, so manoeuvring is done with the throttle, gears and tiller or wheel. Slowing and stopping is done by using reverse gear. With the exception of traditional boats with engine rooms, the throttle and the forward and reverse gears are combined on a single stick.

Boats do not naturally steer accurately in reverse and going backwards successfully is something many boaters never accomplish will great success. (To be fair, some narrowboats have a rear swim shape that

Always remember to slow down when travelling past moored boats or you will get some angry reminders

Taking a boat on a major tidal river like the Thames is not something for the inexperienced boater to tackle

The dramatic Caen Hill Flight of locks on the Kennet and Avon Canal will be mighty hard work but ultimately very rewarding

Dealing with locks is usually simple and fun for all the crew, here closing the upper gate after the boat has entered

The boat waits while the water level is lowered

With the water down, the boat prepares to leave

Rivers, like the Avon here, are wider and faster flowing than canals and levels can change quickly after heavy rain

makes them easier to reverse than others.)

Reversing is best done in straight lines so start by getting the boat in line with the direction you want to travel on the water using the forward gear. Then keep the rudder central and reverse while looking forwards to check it is maintaining its line. (Glance backwards as well of course to check where you are.) If the boat starts to go off line don't try and correct with the tiller, just stop and go forwards to adjust position.

Remember when slowing or reversing that reverse gear is a lower ratio than forwards so you will need a good amount of throttle to spin the prop round and achieve the desired effect.

Turning round can be tricky, too, especially on a narrow canal or anywhere where the waterway is not wide enough to turn around in one manoeuvre. Special turning places – winding holes (prounced as in 'winned' not 'whined') have been dug on narrow canals. Point the bows (the front) of your boat into the apex of the winding hole, then drive the stern of your boat round.

Strong winds can cause problems for any inland waterway craft with a shallow draught and flattish bottom but by being aware of wind direction you can use it to you advantage and avoid difficulties.

For example, use the wind to help turn the boat – drive the boat into the wind at the start of the turn and let the breeze finish the manoeuvre off. When mooring avoid situations where the wind pushes you onto the bank – you might find it hard to get off again, especially in a lighter boat.

Canals are usually still waters, but rivers have currents. You can use this to your advantage when cruising: to help turn the boat around, for example, or to slow it down. When mooring on a river, you will have much more control if you approach from downstream, even if you have to turn around first.

Keep an eye out, too, for flood warning boards, lights, and gauges after rain – fast currents make flooded rivers unsafe for navigation and levels can rise (or fall) overnight while you are moored after heavy rain. You should not attempt tidal rivers until you are an experienced skipper.

LOCKS

Locks are a feature of almost every navigable river or canal, and to be honest, provide most of the fun.

Canal enthusiasts relish the challenge of a busy weekend's locking and avoid canals without them.

The principle behind the lock is simple. The boat enters the lock chamber; the gates are closed behind it; water is let in to raise the boat, or out to lower it; and the gates are opened for the boat to exit.

The water is let in or out via 'paddles' – doors in the chamber walls and gates which are opened by turning a mechanism of cogs and wheels with your windlass. In urban areas, you may also need to unlock the mechanism with a special padlock key. On some waterways there are 'guillotine' locks worked either manually by handle or electrically. On some larger rivers and at various canal locations, the locks are operated for you by full-time lock keepers.

Strong currents are produced as you empty or fill a lock. To be safe, you should always open the paddles in the chamber ('ground paddles') first. Where gate paddles are fitted, open them slowly when the lock is half full. Hook (not tie!) the boat's ropes around the bollards on the lockside, so you can hold it still in the chamber. This is especially important in locks which are wider than the boat.

Staircase locks are a feature of many canals. Here the top gates of one lock are the bottom locks of the next and once you start the sequence you have to keep going up or down. Staircase locks require careful thinking and so that you operate the paddles in the right order, instruction boards are usually provided.

As a general rule you should share a lock with other boats where possible, saving water and time. Steel boats should enter first and leave last when sharing with lighter craft. Wait a few minutes for a boat behind you to catch up, so that you can share. Likewise if the lock is set against you check if there is a boat coming in the other direction before emptying or filling to suit yourself.

When planning your cruise, expect each lock transit to take around 20 minutes. Couple this to an average 3mph cruising speed and you can calculate the time taken to cover a given distance by simply adding the locks and miles together, then dividing by three to get the number of hours.

BRIDGES AND TUNNELS

Canal bridges are usually narrow and tight with room for just one boat at a time – a good test of steering. If your view past the bridge isn't clear then take it steady and prepare to reverse if needs be.

Lift and swing bridges are commonly found. Some are operated by simply pulling on a chain, then holding the bridge open while the boat passes. Others are windlass-operated, or fully mechanised with push-button operation. All require care,

both to hold the bridge open and to minimise delays for road traffic.

Canal tunnels can be over three miles long, not always straight and very dark and wet! A tunnel headlight will provide decent visibility but it can still be tricky to pass another oncoming boat in the gloom. Where a tunnel is too narrow for boats to pass each other, there will usually be a fixed timetable or traffic light system.

It goes without saying that everyone on the boat should stay inboard – tunnel walls are hard and unyielding!

MOORING

Canal towpaths are owned by the navigation authority (usually British Waterways), so you can moor up almost anywhere, except where it is prohibited by signs or clearly unsafe (on a bend or close to a lock).

Riverbanks, on the other hand, are private property, so mooring, except in designated spots provided by the navigation authority or a boating association for members, is at the discretion of the landowner. Local farmers are often obliging; many having 'honesty box' oil drums buried in their field.

Respect their property and don't leave litter, especially anything which could harm animals.

Some boaters worry about mooring in urban areas though often these are safer (if noisier!) than more suburban locations. If in doubt, use official visitor moorings, ask the advice of nearby boaters or speak to a local BW office. For security tie the mooring lines on the boat – some boaters carry chains and locks for secure mooring in 'dodgy' spots.

If you are mooring on a busy river or canal, you can use additional 'springing' lines to hold the boat steady and stop it moving with any turbulence. Run one forwards from the stern and another back from the bow, crossing them over before tying off against a mooring ring or spike.

TRAINING

Finally, though you can learn by experience you can speed the process up and avoid falling into bad habits as well by taking a training course. The RYA administers a one or two day course running through all the basics of boat handling and safety for the Inland Waters Helmsman's Certificate. It can be taken either in your own or a course operator's boat in a number of canal and river locations.

Simple lift bridge are a feature of many canals

Swing bridge amid stunning Pennine scenery

Tunnels come in all lengths and widths but some can be a very tight fit– don't ignore warning barriers

Bridges can be low and tight on many canals, like the Mon & Brec here so mind your heads and your boat

General maintenance

Canal Boat magazine's technical consultant, Tony Brooks, tells students at his boat maintenance courses that the diesel engine is not the main cause of unreliability; people are. And he's right. Here's how not to be a problem owner

An air cooled engine still needs proper winterising

Sometimes you have to get into some tight spots when carrying out engine maintenance jobs

This bay should get a good clean in the winter lay-up

All a diesel engine needs for a long and efficient life is a clean, cool and adequate supply of air; an adequate supply of clean oil; an adequate supply of clean fuel, with no water in it and adequate cooling that is resistant to freezing and causing corrosion. Simple, really.

Problems arise because boats are badly maintained or simply not maintained at all. Even if you don't want to get your hands dirty, an owner who is knowledgeable about the workings of his boat is better placed to foresee problems arising and better able to judge the quality of work being done on their boat.

Like modern cars, modern narrowboats have become increasingly sophisticated and, in many areas, less reliant on owner intervention. Batteries

are sealed for life; engines need only an annual oil change and even the stern gland is now often a sealed, maintenance-free unit. It can all lead to an air of complacency and it is essential to have a routine of checking through the boat to establish that all is well.

But not everyone is fortunate enough to own a new boat; many of us have craft that are ten, twenty even thirty or more years old. And anyone who has owned a thirty-year-old car will know that designed-in reliability and 'fit-and-forget' components did not always play a big part of ownership! Older boats need more routine maintenance and, understandably, closer attention paid to the possibilities of problems through the natural ageing process.

Developing – and sticking to – a sound, regular

maintenance schedule is the key to keeping your boat in good order and highlighting problems before they manifest themselves in a breakdown. The Regular Maintenance panel indicates a typical pattern of routine maintenance.

As you can see from the panel most boats only need the bare minimum of commonsense checks during normal running. The serious maintenance can usually be left to the winter and combined with a winterising or 'lay-up' procedure if the boat is to be left unused.

Proper winterising is a vital part of boat ownership. It takes in three aspects of boat maintenance: firstly, vital servicing to prevent damage during the cold months ahead, second, catching up with problems that have developed over

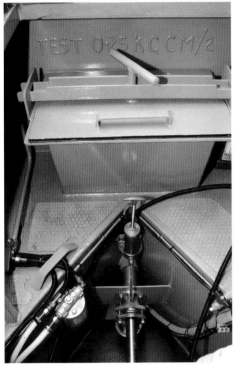

Greaser, fuel filter and weedhatch all need checking

Calorifer, and associated pipes here in engine bay, could need draining if the boat is left unused during a cold winter

Blacking should be re-done and anodes checked

Grease rudder top bearing regularly

Keep battery terminals greased and check charge state

the season and lastly, planning improvements and repairs, rather than waiting for the spring.

A boat that is used will be less likely to deteriorate than one that is closed-up for the winter, so try to make time and effort to visit your boat out-of-season. If possible, take the boat out for a day cruising every month or so as it will reduce damage to the engine and allow the cabin to be dried and ventilated.

ENGINE

The most important and singularly expensive part of the boat that can be damaged by winter frosts and poor maintenance is the engine.

All engines need oil and filter changes carried out to the manufacturer's recommendations but an annual change should be the minimum. Run the engine for a short while to gently warm the oil and make it easier to pump out.

If you have not changed the oil for some time, or often run it off-load to charge the batteries, consider using a flushing oil to remove some of the sludge that may have formed in the sump.

A good clean of the exterior of the main block of the engine, using some washing-up liquid or degreaser and plenty of water, will help spot any future leaks or problem. Run the engine to drive off

any moisture and then rub over with an oily rag to prevent surface corroson.

A fresh-water cooled engine is the most difficult to winterise. The raw water side that takes in canal water must be completely drained, including the water pump. Remove any drain screws on the exhaust system and the cover plate of the water pump. The impellor could be removed (a good time to consider replacement), bagged and hung up over the instrument panel as a reminder not to run the engine! The fresh-water (heat exchanger) side needs to either be drained, or, easier, filled with anti-freeze.

A keel cooled engine, as in narrowboats, needs to be treated with anti-freeze, although the volume needed can be difficult to calculate. A hydrometer (similar, but *not* the same as used for batteries) can show the level of anti-freeze. However, anti-freeze acts not only to prevent damage through freezing but more importantly stops sludging up and corrosion of the engine's internal waterways. For this reason it is generally recommended that keel-cooled engines run on a 50-50 water/anti-freeze mixture. This in turn should be changed at approximately three to five year intervals (longer if the type used allows) and the system reverse flushed through.

Make sure that the engine is worked hard after checking or replenishing anti-freeze levels

(preferably by cruising for a few hours) to make sure that all the solution is circulated properly. Air cooled engines can be squirted with a preserving oil or WD40 into the cooling fan intake as they are shut down. The ducting can be covered with an oily rag or tape to prevent moisture ingress.

The air filter of an engine should be changed as specified (if the replaceable type) or cleaned regularly if the gauze type – the latter by cleaning thoroughly in a strong detergent or paraffin, then drying, followed by soaking in clean engine oil.

If you do visit the boat during the winter then run the engine under load, for at least two hours, to allow any moisture to dissipate and for the sump to become hot.

Keep the fuel tank filled to the brim, to reduce condensation forming. Consider adding a fuel conditioner/water absorber when you fill-up. Drain the fuel filter of water and any sediment. Consider replacing the element, although most engines will then require bleeding – not always an easy process.

BATTERIES

Clean the terminals and posts to bright metal and dress them with petroleum jelly. An "ordinary" lead acid battery should have its electrolyte level checked monthly but as most probably now have catalytic

A picturesque winter scene but the cold can be fatal for your boat's systems unless you take proper precautions

Instantaneous gas water heaters are prone to frost damage unless they are drained down

vent systems it should prove adequate to check it less frequently.

Top up if required with distilled or de-mineralised water to either 3mm above the plates that you can see or to the level indicated on the battery case or by a marker in the topping up hole.

Any battery that needs one or more cells topped up frequently is either being overcharged or is faulty. In adddition, any battery that has its ends bowing out is getting close to the end of its life, so requires watching.

Don't rely on the "magic eye" tester on modern sealed batteries; it only measures the strength of the acid in one cell, although a fault on another is likely to cause a discharged reading eventually. It may also read discharged if the battery has not been topped up sufficiently or has lost liquid through over-charging. Proper testing is done with a hydrometer (on a non-sealed battery) and voltmeter.

Use a quality hydrometer with a number scale as well as coloured zones. Re-charge, ideally off the boat, if the reading is in the red or white zone. If the cell differ by more than 0.05 the battery is probably faulty – take it to a specialist to get this confirmed.

Voltmeter testing is done when the battery is well charged (as at the end of a normal running day). The surfaces of a battery's plates become fully charged well before the rest of the plates and this 'surface charge' must be eliminated to avoid false readings before voltmeter testing.

Spin the engine on the starter for 30 seconds or so (with the stop out) to clear that battery. Domestic battery banks are far more difficult: the larger the bank the more difficult. Running a shower or water pump for ten minutes or so is one option.

Then connect a voltmeter set to 20V DC (200V

DC for 24 volt boats) across the bank and take a reading.

More than 12.5v indicates fully charged, 12.2 to 12.5v is half charged and less than 12.2v means deeply discharged. At the end of the day one would expect more than 12.5v, if you have less, either the battery is faulty or the charging system is faulty.

STERN GLAND

The stern tube should be repacked or tightened if large quantities of grease have to be used to prevent drips at the end of the day. It can be a DIY job but is one area where it is very important to seek professional help if you are unsure. A failure here could lead to catastrophic consequences.

While in the engine space grease threads on the weedhatch and check the gasket seal. Does any floatswitch on the bilge pump work? Spray any exposed wiring and terminals with WD40 and grease all grease nipples. Grease the bearing for the rudder – most modern ones have a grease nipple – use stern tube grease, and place a rag around the top of the bearing as you apply the grease to force more down the tube.

OUTSIDE

Wash the paintwork down. Consider a marine wax if you have an expensive or decorative paint scheme. An overall cover may increase the lifespan of the paintwork, but won't do much for the rest of the boat by reducing ventilation, so is probably not a good idea.

Fitted covers to cratches and semi-trad/cruiser aft deck do need to be cleaned thoroughly (with a mild detergent made for the job – not washing-up liquid) and treated with a specific preserver. Doing this before winter sets in can

greatly reduce damage during the winter.

Consider giving the cruising ropes a good wash at home; put the ropes in old pillowcases, and wash using a non-biological liquid detergent on the lowest setting on your machine. This can remove grit which shortens the life of the ropes and reduce damage to the paintwork.

Now is a good time to cover up minor scratches in the paintwork – both topsides and hull. Even a quick rub-down with sand paper and a single coat of enamel or bitumen will slow down corrosion and reduce the chores in the summer.

Clean, de-rust and re-paint all external lockers. If your hosepipe is stowed in a locker, make sure it is drained, or it may be damaged by frost. Lubricate all exterior locks, hinges, catches and runners.

Hull blacking is often carried out in winter – every second season generally suffices. Having the boat hauled out on a slipway or in a dry dock and pressure-washed for blacking is also an opportunity to check the condition of the hull and anodes.

INSIDE

The water system is the most likely to be damaged. Empty the tank as much as possible with the water pump. Potable water anti-freeze is available from chandlers, and very useful if the boat is not going to be used during the winter – the system is partly filled and the solution drawn through all the taps. Do not consider using engine anti-freeze: this is toxic! Otherwise, all low points need to be free of water, especially the pump itself. Calorifiers must be emptied and instantaneous hot water heaters have the drain-plug removed as they are particularly vulnerable.

Low level runs of pipework (below the waterline) are less likely to be frozen, but consider dismantling any dips in the pipes where water may accumulate. Leave taps open and take care with draining shower fittings. Make sure that the shower evacuation pump is dry: consider removing the hoses from either side.

Clean bilges of debris so that damp can evaporate or drain towards any bilge pump (and check operation of float valves on these.)

Pump-out toilets should be emptied and flushed out well. Whether you leave toilet chemical in the

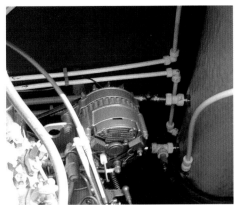

Drain down the calorifier in winter via the drain tap provided at the base of the unit

The in-line fuel filter traps water and sediment and should be cleaned or emptied as required

The skin tank vent can be opened to bleed air from the cooling system when replenishing or re-filling

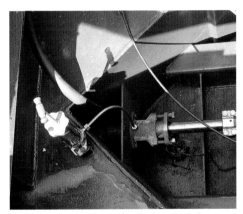

The stern gland needs regular checking for leakage – here a bilge pump protects against possible flooding

holding tank over winter is personal preference, but more will have to be added when the boat is used, as it looses its potency. Porta-Potti type toilets should be completely drained, including the flushing pump and left with the valves open/lid off. Any freshwater connection needs to be drained, along with flushing mechanisms. Consider wiping a thin amount of olive oil (with a tissue) on the seals of some toilets to keep them supple – check maker's manual.

Radiator central heating systems can be treated with anti-freeze the same way as an engine. Again, ensure they are run to distribute the fluid – bleed radiators too.

Open a few windows, if the hopper-type, to encourage good ventilation. Do not cover any vents – movement of air is vital to stave off damp. Leave cupboard doors ajar, turn bedding on its side and open up lockers. Consider replacing decent curtains with a cheap winter set, to avoid condensation damage. Remove anything from the galley that could go off, or attract rodents. Bottled water, tonic, and beer etc. may freeze and burst. Wipe all surfaces with a mild disinfectant and open fridge doors to prevent mildew.

SECURITY

Visit the boat often! Fit good-quality locks, hasps and staples. Make your boat looks secure. Consider a cheap, but effective burglar alarm. Remove any valuable and especially portable items such as DVD players or TVs. Mark everything else with the boat's

name, or, better still, index number. Make sure the boat is well-secured to the bank and fendered sufficiently to allow to movement. Set the boat to spring lines in addition to fore-and-aft mooring, to reduce scraping of the hull. Check stoppage notices to see if there could be a dramatic change of water level, such as locks or a pound being closed.

REFITTING

The springtime refit is the opposite of laying up, which is fine in theory but if you have opened draincocks or switched off systems during the lay-up make sure you have noted these down rather than finding out when water laps round your feet or the engine temperature sky-rockets!

WINTER JOBS

It is a good idea during your cruising season to keep a note book in which to record the things that will need attention – like sorting out loose hinges, changing door/drawer handles, tightening hinges and so on. You can also record a wish list of improvements you want to make. Come winter, you'll have plenty to keep yourself busy!

In the same book note such things as filter and other service part numbers (to save the cost of buying identical products through expensive outlets), basic technical data such as sizes, current draws of electrical items, capacities, pump types and so on, as well as the location of pipe and cable runs. It is all part of knowing your boat and being prepared.